# HIS BLOOD REIGNS FOREVER

## The Power Within the Blood Covenant

*Mary Anna Burriss*

His Blood Reigns Forever
ISBN: 0-88144-353-0
Copyright © 2008 by Mary Anna Burriss

Published by
VICTORY PUBLISHING
A Division of Yorkshire Publishing Group
7707 East 111th Street South, Suite 104
Tulsa, Oklahoma 74133
www.yorkshirepublishing.com

# Contents

# A Note to You, Reader, from the Author

This book is a bit unique in that it flows in a liberated style of writing! Imagine you're taking a few days relaxation time for just your body, eating at one **feeding** place and in God's wisdom **balancing** your best food intake for every part! You're walking along by an enormous buffet or smorgasbord daily. Your purpose is to enjoy the right foods to contribute to your inner health, others to act as a dynamic **catalyst** to stimulate energy, some to be like an **oasis** for refreshing your body, and others to aid in digestion, respiration, circulation and everything else. As you're walking by the buffet, you can watch a variety of action dramas revealing the value of certain foods about which you may be unaware.

Connecting in the spiritual realm, you will see there will be numerous experiences (food) for your **spirit,** so the Holy Spirit will reveal understanding of the value of the Blood and the Covenant in His Blood for you. Salted throughout are autobiographical incidents to help **amplify Scriptural facts.** On these you may desire to **meditate** Josh. 1:8 and digest them rather than rush right through to get done with the reading. In the Hebrew language, the word **meditate** even means to mutter at times. You might want to read one chapter and set it aside in order to study the Bible with the Teacher Himself!

Readers, please enjoy allowing your spirits to overflow with Grace, Shalom and Joy as the Word brings greater wisdom, understanding, depth and love for the **Better Covenant** and the **Living Blood** of Jesus!

# Dedication

There are **not enough** adequate words in English **to express** my **thankfulness** in depth to **Almighty God** for revealing **Jesus,** then **Himself** and the **Holy Spirit** in many ways. They have taught me through so many creative ways in a still small voice or a dynamically bold word; through interesting or difficult experiences; through trials and pitfalls; through simply living and more; through numerous saints with dynamic callings depositing golden nuggets; through many, many prophecies; the list is never-ending! Yet **every** occasion has been a springboard for enrichment in knowing more about Jesus and becoming more like Him, when I apply the Written Word!

God has displayed His Love in **unfathomable** ways **every** day of my life, though not always recognized by me! Always and **only** by invitation He has led me to teach the gamut of His Word from four-to-ninety year olds, about His precious Blood, the Holy Spirit, sneaky enemy tactics, prayer, statutes and principles from His Written Word. I have taught, blessed and delivered in several business places, in homes and in churches. He has permitted me in conjunction with Him to minister to many others!

Daddy God has answered all my questions in His wisdom countless times with revelation and in surprising ways, **His.** He has sustained my health for eighty plus years and has prompted me to write and publish two books, for which He has brought in **all** the financial needs. His calling has been beyond what I ever imagined. My **heart** prayer is that His words, as well as those of Jesus and the Holy Spirit, will **richly** and **deeply Bless every person** who will read all or any portion of this book!

My everlasting thanks to You, Father God, for my Covenant Partner, **John,** for more than fifty years. Together, we have persevered and believed in the reality and basic importance of the **Better Covenant** between Abba Father, Jesus and the Holy Spirit demonstrated in two **totally opposite** personalities! Enjoy Ephesians 5:17-23. We believed in a permanent relationship "'til death do us part," despite the fact that our revelation was very simple, lacking the **depth** of **continuing** revelation that is still unfolding today! My only requirement for a Husband was one who loved Father, Son and Holy Spirit, who would allow me to teach our children about Jesus Whom I deeply loved, and therefore someone who would remain **faithful** to **His Covenant!** He surely has! Way to go, Hubby!

This gentleman wears a **Life Crown** for his **B.A. Event,** "Born Again in Christ" combined with the **Ph.D.** for the "Power to Heal and Deliver others," including his Master's Calling to stay on **His** path, as he has and **still is,** by **diligently** working for **seeds** to plant in Daddy God's work; a three-in-one Hat for Husband, Father and Grandfather; a Navy Hat for our rough and tumultuous seasons; a UPS Hat for pick ups and deliveries of frequent and varied needs for my first, and this book; a Nehemiah's Hat for building and rebuilding parts of a fence, benefiting four other neighbors' lawns as well; a Grocery and Drug Store Deliverer's Hat for all items needed even if at peculiar hours; a Repairman's Hat for the myriad of items he fixes, often resulting in inventing a few missing parts; and a Painter's Hat for indoors and outdoors! He wears his **choice** hats as well — Boeing, AWACS, a Target Hat for accurate pistol shooting, a Cowboy Hat and last but vitally important a Conductor's Hat because of his love of steam trains, especially! Thanks oodles and oodles, Hubby!

This is also dedicated to my first-born, daughter Suzanna and her husband Saúl; my second-born, son John and his wife, Tricia; and their two sons, my grandsons, Joshua and Steven! They are absolutely heart desired, miracle love gifts and encouragers, who love Father God, Jesus and the Holy Spirit! In addition, to Marilyn Vannoy, who has become a friend "who sticks closer than a sister," which I never had, and who has **served** and **assisted** willingly, diligently and joyfully with books and **significantly** more! To the children, women and men friends, who have received my Bible teaching and have done innumerable generous and unselfish things for our family, far more than we could ask or think.

Also this is dedicated to the Beloved Readers, every one of you, whom I pray and believe will **celebrate Father, Son (Jesus)** and the **Holy Spirit** and all the **riches** given to us as eternal gifts! May you be renewed, reinforced, re-fired and enhanced as you see and hear more about the "10Kingdom of our God, authority of his Messiah! The Accuser of our brothers and sisters thrown out, who accused them day and night before God. 11They defeated him through the blood of the Lamb, and the bold word of their witness. They weren't in love with themselves; they were willing to die for Christ." Revelation 12 The Message

# Introduction

Have you any idea of the **value** of the physical **blood** in your own body, since you and I are so "fearfully *and* wonderfully made?" Psalm 139:14 In fact the Amplified version of the Bible speaks so clearly and stunningly, "15My frame was not hidden from You, when I was being formed in secret *and* intricately *and* curiously wrought (as if embroidered with various colors) in the depths of the earth [a region of darkness and mystery]. 16Your eyes saw my unformed substance, and in Your book all the days *of my life* were written, before ever they took shape, when as yet there was none of them."

This Scripture passage reveals so much about God's love for us, and how He wanted each of us to be **born,** no matter what **anyone** else says about us, even parents sometimes, and especially Satan! **You** are **not** an accident! Almighty God desired you and still wants **you** here. He has an earthly plus eternal plan for **you,** which was written in Heaven in His book **before** you were even conceived. When you invite Jesus into your heart, you are born into the Body of Christ, a large family, with your **individually** created and designed assignment or calling from God. Ephesians 1:18 His **perfect will** for you is revealed progressively as you walk closely with Jehovah. Romans 12:2 If that is not an **awesome** and **incomprehensible truth,** then to me there is no actual truth revealed anywhere.

His plans are not on the spur-of-the-moment plans, but infinitely wrought for each and every possible situation: an example is when Adam **betrayed** God with his decision and disobedience. God **already** knew what He must do to keep all those who would be a part of His enormous family **now** and for **eternity!** John 10:28-30 Now in **His** heart, **Blood** is vitally important and essential in this enormous plan. The word **blood** is found **338 times** in the Old Covenant, which shadows its importance in the New Covenant, pointing to the Lamb of God, the Lord Jesus Christ, crucified before the foundation of the world. Revelation 13:8

The word **blood** is found **101 times** in the New and Better Covenant! So since it is so much a part of God's heart, so interwoven as a basis in His covenants, it seems very wise spiritually, mentally, emotionally and bodily to know some of the awe-inspiring truths about blood! This includes knowing about blood covenants in the Western world as the Eastern world is already more knowledgeable. Every nation on this earth, no matter if primitive or not, has some basic understanding about covenant. God's children, which we are if Jesus is our Lord, need to have a deeper understanding of covenant, because God takes it so very seriously and **He initiated** this plan with mankind! Do you know Satan lived very close to Almighty God Jehovah Isaiah 14:12 before he rebelled? Luke 10:18 At some point in time, it's revealed he reeked with pride! I believe that is one reason his hatred of God results in attempts "to steal, and to kill, and to destroy" John 10:10 every covenant, particularly in marriages!

Why are **some** offended so seriously by this precious word, even to the extent that some churches have removed **all** the **blood hymns** from their song books and **the Cross** from the **church buildings?** Why, when God's love was demonstrated so powerfully through His dear Son, Jesus, by shedding **all** His Blood and redeeming mankind — you and me? Realize the **Cross** announces and declares Jesus to the world and our real belief in Him. Have we become so haughty or intellectual that we're attempting to judge Almighty God? **May it not be so!** As a part of the Body of Christ have these churches denied Jesus and abdicated their eternal Life connection to God?

**All** our **good** deeds and **kindnesses,** no matter how they are regarded by the world are **dead works,** Hebrews 9:14 without our Master's initiating them and receiving the Glory! Are they ashamed of the foundation of the Gospel? 1 Corinthians 3:11 Then there can be no Gospel. For on that **Cross** God was sowing the **most precious Seed** He had, His only virgin begotten Son! Matthew 1:23 On the **Cross** and prior to the Cross for hours as well, where Christ endured such heinous abuse, afterwards conquering hell, defeating Satan and all his devils, taking the keys of death, hell and the grave, "He made a public spectacle of them, triumphing over them in it." Colossians 2:15 For whom? For **every** single person who has lived, who is living, and those yet to be born! John 3:14 17

Do you see therefore **why** Father God never wants any of His creation to go to hell? Yes, the event was so dynamic, traumatic, yet victorious, it **never** can be equaled, nor are there any adequate, superlative words in English to describe all Jesus accomplished! My desire for willing readers who listen is to dispel **completely** that offense and such dreadful **words** against God! Let's remember words are containers! **Containers of life or death!** Proverbs 18:21

Beloved Reader, let's see what we can discover about **blood** that will cause us to **see** and **know** in a crystal-clear way Its value cannot be measured. Therefore we must not discard It! Jehovah God revealed to Moses in the law that "You shall partake of the blood of no kind of flesh, for the life of all flesh is its blood." Leviticus 17:14 AMP How enormously important this command from God is, since He does not want us eating the **life** of man or animal. This was God's instruction to the Israelites, but is obviously for us as well because of the Blood Covenant and our being engrafted into the Vine, Jesus.

In the New Testament, when Jesus introduced communion, He being the Written Word made flesh, John 1:1, 14 must have shocked the Jewish people, but He was revealing progressively that He is "the Way and the Truth and the Life; no one comes to the Father except by (through) Me," John 14:6 AMP and they were to **partake** (drink) of the Written Word spiritually and **eat** resurrected life, the Word of God.

Also, do you know that your blood is **not** just a liquid, but it is **tissue,** the only tissue that **moves throughout** your body? I call it much richer in substance then, because it accomplishes a great deal more in your body than a liquid could! Also, that your **body dies,** not your spirit nor your soul, the very minute your **blood stops flowing.** We will learn, too, that Almighty God has His Heavenly Court where the Blood of Jesus already reigns supreme with the Trinity, I believe. I capitalize the Blood of Jesus because It is alive and speaks!

I'll reveal more later. However **know** that every person living **never** dies: they either graduate to Heaven or fail God's choice for them and go to hell — **not** by God's choice but **as a result** of **his or her own decision!** This is not my opinion, which would be of no value, but is the **truth** in the Bible. Doesn't **sanctified** common sense reveal we don't plan to have children and then send them on purpose to eternal damnation, where pain is so intense and never ceases? Know Almighty **God is perfect Love.** I recall a dear radio preacher used to say frequently, if you disagree with God leave, find or make your own planet. Exactly! Our only wise conclusion, Father God knows what is best for each of us and that is His heart!

# CHAPTER 1

## Imagination and Creativity Are God's Gifts!

Where God's love is prevalent His **creativity** abounds and abounds. It is even seen in the surprise of children's ability to make a toy out of a cardboard box or a hiding place under a card table and a sheet. When young I made puppets from Mom's wooden clothespins which were just split apart and a simplistic puppet stage built out of rags and boxes!

Often **young** children from two or three years old if allowed and encouraged **will** accept Jesus into their **hearts!** In fact I recall when a five year old boy was asked how he knew Jesus was there, answered, "Because I shut the door and **locked** it, so He can't get away!" Please don't squelch these comments, because of a child's lack of deep under-standing. The Holy Spirit accomplishes the impossible, so He will take care of development after conception.

Years ago when I was teaching four year olds in Sunday school, we had a unrehearsed afternoon program for the parents, where I used a picture of Jesus with children painted by Richard Hook! We just shared like we were in class, as the Spirit led and momentum built until I asked, "What would you do if Jesus came in the door right **now** and walked down the aisle?" One child started to say something but a second little girl burst out, "I'd **kiss** Him!" The class **erupted** with abundant and refreshing joy, which spilled onto the parents.

My heart's desire is that you will ask Almighty God to enhance **your** imagination and **creativity** as you read this **freely,** not expecting or demanding a structured form. It is not. So again, may God's glorious wisdom, peace, joy and understanding ripple into your spirit, perhaps surprising you with new "ideas, concepts and insights" as Oral Roberts once said! Beloved Reader, **many times** the enemy has deceived human beings by erasing, discrediting or destroying their creativity or imagination. Let each of us **invite** God to reign over our spirit, soul and body!

# CHAPTER 2

# Let's Fast-Forward ... Take a Peek

Have you ever pondered why Jesus' Blood was shed completely and yet still is **living**, is **anointed** and is actively **accomplishing** works outside of Christ's body? Since His Blood is alive, you will see It capitalized on purpose! His Blood is personified. Why Satan and his followers can have no understanding about His Blood is partially because he's never had any, therefore the results are his **total fear** of It, hatred and lies against It.

One **exciting** incident related to me by a young friend who knew of some of my victorious experiences with the Blood comes to mind. He and the boy's father were led by the Holy Spirit to cast out evil spirits from his nephew, an **autistic** child, whom I believe was about six years old. One evil spirit spoke through the child, saying, "Stop using the Blood. It's **hot!**" I asked my friend, "What did you do, pour more on?" (This means declare and decree, utilizing the word **Blood** and appropriate Scriptures.) He said, "Yes, we did!"

After two or three sessions, led by the Holy Spirit, the nephew's schoolteacher noticed a tremendous difference in his behavior in class, so she dismissed him from her **specialized** class! Just like the Bible says, **instant** success results when done by the Holy Spirit through you in faith and in the power of the Scriptures! Lester Sumrall, a man of "great faith" in God Matthew 8:10 and amazing obedience, was able to bring forth extremely heavy and mighty deliverances from very wicked spirits — even a **ruling** spirit in a 17 year old girl in Bilibid Prison in Manila, Philippines, resulting in an awesome revival over many years! *Alien Entities, Volume 1, pgs 54-56* by Dr. Lester Sumrall He stated once in a class taught by him on a video I saw that "he never came against the enemy without using the **Blood** of **Jesus** as a **hammer!**" You see **It** is a wonderfully, powerfully commanding **force** against the enemy! Yippeeee!

One other experience I had revealed the enemy's attempt to stop proceedings against his trickery, by trying to distract several ladies and me. We were ministering to a distraught woman in a deliverance session, and I was looking up a demon's name from Scripture in a reliable Biblical workbook, when an **impudent male** voice came from her, asking, "What are you doing with that dumb book?" My reply was not as respectful as it should have been, perhaps, for God did create the angels, who rebelled following Satan's leading, Matt. 25:41 but I replied, "Getting rid of a dumb demon like you." Almost instantly the upset lady turned to another one in our team and **seductively** uttered in that same male voice, "You're so pretty!" (She is prettier than I.) But the demons were surely **trying to** distract at least one of us! However their skullduggery failed.

Thanks be to Almighty God our focus stayed on track during the session mentioned above! This is very essential when delivering people since the demons can talk, Matt. 8:28-32 argue incessantly, lie of course, John 8:44 deceive and distract you cunningly. Be very alert, **know** you have the **authority** given by Jesus and remain on constant guard, if you are willing to be involved in obeying the Great Commission from Jesus in Mark 16:15-18! It is very helpful to go with at least one other person who **fears not,** of course, since you can be mentored and assist one another, as the Holy Spirit leads! You do not have to know the name of the demon(s). Sometimes you will, but don't waste time asking or talking with the demons; do get your total leading from the Holy Spirit! John 14:26 He knows and cannot be fooled.

In our home another time, a young mother was with a group of women who were studying some of the Scriptures and she suddenly blurted out, "I want to accept Jesus as my Lord and be baptized in the Holy Spirit. But **I can't.**" This was a brief time after I had been baptized, but out of me came "I know what to do, it has to be a demon." The minute we cast it out, she was able to accept Jesus and His Baptism of the Holy Spirit and fire! Matt. 3:11 Later we did more praying and deliverance, as she had many Mormons in her family whom she **dearly** loved.

Satan's pride has cost him eternal absence from Almighty God's presence Isaiah 14:12-15 and he fights persistently against God and everything dear to His heart! Angels are not given revelation at all, so cannot understand about the awesomeness of man and Almighty God's **incomparable love, grace** and **mercy** for man and all He has invested in him either! Hebrews 2:6-7 Therefore demons surely cannot understand the blood physically, let alone the **matchless** importance of the Blood of Jesus in God's heart and **spiritually** to the Body of Christ! Physically the blood is our **life line** to living on earth, for if it stops flowing, you're a goner. Spiritually the Blood of Jesus is the **life line** of the Body of Christ. How can It still be alive?

Another time when I was ministering on the phones for The 700 Club, a woman called and was fascinated and yet fearful by what she called **God's** actions, when her bed slid by itself from one end of the room to the other! I had to correct her led by the Holy Spirit to say, "This was not God; let's clean out your room spiritually!" She became irate and wanted to stick to what she had **deceptively** believed. When I asked her "What purpose was accomplished?" She had no answer.

God **always** has a **purpose** for what He does to accomplish a part of His **superior** plan in His wonderful, matchless wisdom. It would

19

never be for foolishness, nor to attract attention nor appear spectacular, yet it might be for a demonstration of His power in His Word. It could seem strange and even surprising sometimes, but test the spirit by asking Him and mind the knowing within your own spirit, now quickened and occupied by His Holy Spirit. 1 John 4:1 Because the purposes of Jehovah God can be so **extensive,** so are His **anointings,** as **He** wills! Some of you may **feel** or **sense** His anointing in your body but that is not His purpose, for the anointings are of the Holy Spirit and we are to **yield** and **follow,** to **break bondages** and **destroy yokes.** Isa. 10:27

At one time my heart was touched by a young believer with cancer when I was young in the spirit. Suddenly I was quickened with **waves** of anointing from head to toe and directed to see him; I started to call the hospital, but was told to phone his home! The Holy Spirit told me which family to call, and I went there, boldly and unstoppable. My neighborhood lady went with me, where we introduced ourselves to his parents, was told he was **asleep,** so we prayed with the parents and left! But I missed the mission for he was to have been healed. It was a moment in time for God and me. I repented deeply.

Years later I was attending a church in a medium-sized warehouse, after we had been praising God, when I was catapulted with an anointing to run down one aisle, across the back and the other aisle to my seat. Never have I been a runner but I do believe God was demonstrating Himself for someone there! His power is **awesome!** Remember **Elijah's** amazing speed run? 1 Kings 18:46 But I do not look for any repeat anointings but freely expect what He might want.

So now together you, the Holy Spirit, Jesus and God indwelling in **oneness** in you and me John 15:4-5, 7; 17:21 are going on an adventure that will take you to heights you may never have contacted before perhaps or you may start knowing more about our complexity in God's creativeness. You will be enriched and refreshed or attain richer understanding from Almighty God which you have longed for in your heart! You will be "more than conquerors" Romans 8:37 and more accurate "doers" of the Word of God. James 1:22 Fasten your seat belt and ride on the wings of an eagle, because together we will be seeing anew and experiencing increased tastes of God as well as tromping on, exterminating, therefore utterly destroying the lies of our enemy! Be **expectant** to receive and change, because you may have an area or two where deception has crept in as if on cat's feet into your life.

# CHAPTER 3

# Catalyst for Mind Renewal

There are so many amazing secrets and truly awesome treasures hidden until these last days, which are now being revealed because of God's Glory and heart's desire that we scarcely can catch our breath. Remember the song several decades ago called *All Over the World the Spirit is Moving*, based on Habakkuk 2:14? It's truly under way mightily right now, as I'm writing! Reality and fulfillment!

First of all, let's review some of the main events shortly after Jesus was crucified and appeared to His followers on earth. Do you recall Mary Magdalene, whom Jesus had delivered of seven demons, Mark 16:9 obviously very grateful for His ministry to her, was by the tomb crying because the body of Jesus was gone. John 20:11 How she had changed and loved Him with such **pure** love, *agapé*. But there He stood in His glorified body when He spoke to her, "Stop clinging to Me, for not yet have I ascended to the Father, but be on your way to My brethren and say to them, I am ascending to My Father and your Father and My God and your God." John 20:17 Wuest Even though He had to correct her action, He very lovingly gave her a **special** mission to perform! Are you aware of why He was ascending to the Father?

Father God wanted that **precious Blood** Jesus had shed, still **living** today, to be brought to Heaven to accomplish a miraculous event there. Heb. 9:23 This was hidden in the Old Testament in Exodus, Ch. 24 when Moses was commanded by God to affirm the covenant to sprinkle blood on the altar; next he read "the Book of the Covenant" to reveal to the people what they were to obey; then the blood was sprinkled on the people; later the blood and the anointing oil were sprinkled on the priests and their garments; Ch. 29 still later it was sprinkled seven times before the veil, separating the **Holy** of holies Leviticus 4 prophesying the **restoration** of Father God's relationship with His children through Jesus and His precious Blood! Heb. 9:18-22 Do you realize we in the Body of Christ are kings and priests? Rev. 1:6

Another foretelling revealed hundreds of years later by James in chapter 2:13 is written, "Mercy triumphs over judgment." After Jesus delivered His Blood to Almighty God, He cleansed the utensils in the heavenlies with His Blood, thus consecrating them anew, as revealed in the book of Hebrews chapter 9. He still continually **cleanses** our sins **completely,** the second they are confessed! Can you understand now why animals' blood was also sprinkled on the mercy seat? It is so wonderful that God covered or atoned for the sins of the Old Testament Saints, (to be revealed) which were confessed only **once yearly,** Heb. 9:6-7 but it would be most difficult and discouraging to see a long list of sins, knowing the minute you sinned, the list would start again and they were **not removed** but only **covered over** with animals' blood!

What a **Blessing** we have in our Better Covenant, **unbreakable,** made **between God** and **Jesus,** Galatians 3:15-18 for we can confess our sins immediately the **second** we're aware of them! Our sins are **eradicated** 1 John 1:9 with **anointed, living Blood** — no appointment needed, no voice mail, no call waiting, no email, no tired cell phones and in addition **no list** is made nor is **condemnation** ever spewed out from our **loving** Father! Almighty God deliberately forgets our sins, Jeremiah 31:34; Heb. 8:12; 10:17 besides forgiving them on the spot, the **very second** they are confessed. In addition He gives us the heart desire, the power and the ability, to cease sinning once we come to Jesus and ask Him to be Lord and Savior of our lives. Rom. 10::9-10 Glory to God! **Alleluia!**

Because the Blood purifies so completely, **It** can be applied in many ways, confounding the enemy and his tribe utterly. **It** can be applied on our eyes for blinded deception, in the ears for deadened hearing, on our tongues to free them to speak a heavenly prayer language, to soften hard hearts, to help in restoring a "conscience seared," 1 Timothy 4:2 KJV to cleanse brains, memories and spirits, to assist in **eliminating** unwanted evil ideas, ugly memories, flashbacks, hurtful sights and images, traumatic events, perverted actions and words of dreadful death spoken to us or even by us before we knew better! A seared conscience in the Greek means cauterized!

Next, God's wisdom would tell us to consult the Holy Spirit immediately for a Scripture to **speak boldly** and **loudly,** slamming the door closed on any possible entrance by the enemy into us! The power is still in the **spoken** Word. As members of God's family, the Body of Christ, don't we believe Proverbs 18:21? "Death and life are in the power of the tongue, and they who indulge it shall eat the fruit of it [for death or life]." AMP In our day I've been stunned at the quantity and definitely polluted, totally destructive words spoken within many family units, where Love, Life of Jesus and Light should permeate the atmosphere, because it pours out of us, affecting us and those closest to us, as well as **entire** neighborhoods and cities, even His divine appointments in individual situations. "Now hope does not disappoint, because the love of God has been poured out in our hearts by the Holy Spirit who was given to us." Rom. 5:5 So we are **atmosphere** changers for excellence and deep respect for individuals, God's creation!

Do you remember what **Jesus** said in Matthew 12? "35A good man out of the good treasure of his heart brings forth good things, and an evil man out of the evil treasure brings forth evil things. 36But I say to you that for every idle word men may speak, they will give account of it in the day of judgment. 37For by your words you will be justified, and by your words you will be condemned." The Amplified Bible says in verse 35, "and the evil man out of his inner evil storehouse flings forth evil things." The visible anger and hatred toward loved ones is truly incomprehensible. Also in Ephesians 4:29, AMP "Let no foul *or* polluting language, *nor* evil word, *nor* unwholesome *or* worthless talk [ever] come out of your mouth; but only such [speech] as is good *and* beneficial to the spiritual progress of others, as is fitting to the need *and* the occasion, that it may be a blessing *and* give grace (God's favor) to those who hear it."

By the way, according to *Vine's Expository Dictionary of Biblical Words, New Testament Words,* pg 104 the verb "cleanse (1) 'means to make clean, to cleanse' (a)from physical stains and dirt ... Matt. 23:25 ... ; from disease, as of leprosy; Matt. 8:2; (b)in a moral sense, from the defilement of sin, Acts 15:9; ... ; 'cleanse' from the guilt of sin, Eph. 5:26; 1 John 1:7; ... . " In addition it means purging and purifying, so when our sins are cleansed they are truly forever "out of sight," gone forever, kaput, vamoose skied, "as far as the east is from the west." Psalm 103:12 How can the east ever meet the west? Wonderfully it cannot! Whoopee! In addition, Almighty God has **chosen** to **forget** them **on purpose!** (I mentioned this earlier.) Isn't that astounding? Think of how much that Blesses us, that Almighty God, Who is perfect, knows all, is Creator of all, has perfect recall and deliberately **forgives** and **forgets all** our sins, law breaking and iniquities! Can you believe it? This is a good place to shout thanks to God.

The extra Blessing of this is that Satan has nothing to back up his accusations regarding our past (one of his favorite tactics) because Almighty God has **eradicated** them. When I was young in grade school, we dipped our pens in an inkwell when we were writing; honestly, there was no such thing as an ink-filled pen, and there was an extremely effective ink **eradicator** liquid for any mistakes we made. I mean they were gone really (no comparison to our current Wite-Out, which only **covers** or acts like a coating). I compare our current Wite-Out to the **atonement** for sins **only** in the **Old** Testament Covenants and the ink eradicator to **cleansing** our sins in the **New** Testament Covenant.

The Scripture in Isaiah 43:25, the Lord God is speaking and says, "I, *even* I, *am* He who blots out your transgressions for My own sake; and I will not remember your sins." The word "blot" in Hebrew is "machah" which means "to wipe, to wipe off, to blot out; to adjoin, touch on; to be wiped out, to be wiped off, to be removed, to be effaced, to be destroyed; to be smeared with fat; to put away." This definition is found in the *Hebrew Greek Key Study Bible, pg 1605* the Zodhiates' original and complete system of Bible study.

How marvelous even in the Old Testament God was preparing a pathway for His children to defeat the enemy. We **must** realize and appreciate the miraculous phenomenon and power of the Blood accomplishing this, in order to be brought into a maturity in Christ and appreciation of the depth of the Blood's value. Heb. 13:20-21 Accepting this truth also closes and seals the door shut to one of the ways the enemy plunges in with accusations of past sins. Our part to assure this is to repent quickly of our sins with a heart desire to **change** our **mind!** Rom. 12:1-2

Would you meditate now to see the **real** magnificence of this in your walk in the Spirit, so it becomes a **rhema** word in you for a deeper appreciation and more revelation. In 1 John 1:9 it is an **instantaneous** cleansing by the Blood, so we're cleansed **rapidly** as we confess, thereby keeping a **squeaky** clean daily walk in the spirit. See why Satan needs **to try** to squelch — "to steal, and to kill, and to destroy" John 10:10 — the Blood songs and revelations about **It** in the hymn books, as well as convince the churches to get rid of the **Cross?!** These are absolutely essential to redemption!

In fact even as I write this, on the news in April 2008 the Eastside Baptist Church, located in Tacoma, Washington, was burned except for **one wall** on which a **Cross** was mounted! This was visible even from the air. God will bring beauty out of ashes, as they rebuild it, I am certain. Isa. 61:3-4 To me that is a miracle of God exclaiming the **reality** of Redemption! Psychology, philosophy, lofty thinking, reasonings, traditions of men and on and on won't and can't cut it. 2 Corinthians 10:4-5 We must not continue attempting to use corruptible **wormy** bread **seed** mixed in with **incorruptible** Bread of Heaven, our precious Lord Jesus. 1 Peter 1:22-23; Heb. 4:12 It promotes confusion and discredits Jehovah and the Lord Jesus.

Amazing! Have you ever experienced Satan attempting to pull you backwards into miry darkness, so he could keep you constantly spinning your wheels, spiraling downward into dark despondency or pedaling backwards, getting nowhere fast or even worse imparting lies about what your ugly doom will be in your **future? I have!** In fact, early on as a **spiritual child** in learning to walk in the spirit, I'd sit at home and **verbally** beat myself intermittently for days when I made mistakes, especially publicly. Finally I heard God tell me, the reason it **was** made public was because I continued **reinforcing** it by **saying** that is what happened — I was reaping what I was sowing! Gal. 6:7

I recall once prophesying in a song at a meeting, stepping out there in faith and realizing I was completely off. I stopped in mid-air! It was a dreadful realization to say the least, but mistakes will occur and we can learn much from them, but not by plopping down in a corner, pouting, hiding and wallowing in self-pity and sympathy, retracting ourselves into a shell like the head of a huge turtle, plus dwelling on self. Yuck!

We must beware because this is in direct disobedience to Philippians 3:13-15. "13Brethren, I do not count myself to have apprehended; but one thing *I do*, forgetting those things which are behind and reaching forward to those things which are ahead, 14I press toward the goal for the prize of the upward call of God in Christ Jesus. 15Therefore let us, as many as are mature, have this mind; and if in anything you think otherwise, God will reveal even this to you." For the race we're running on earth is to **focus — meditate day** and **night** on the Written Word Joshua 1:8 and Jesus, the Written Word made flesh among us. John 1:14 Also, our God is a God of continual increase in **every facet** of our lives, with restoration and refreshing, **faithful** gifts, if we follow Jesus! This requires constant and diligent work. I call it checkmating yourself for **it is** possible. What a way to fly!

This immature behavior was prior to my knowing Jesus **took** all our embarrassment and shame on the Cross! Isa. 53; Heb. 12:2 Jesus also exchanged sympathy for ourselves, to our reaching out in powerful, endless **compassion** in action for others, 1 Pet. 3:8; 2 Corinth. 1:4 if we are willing. Before Jesus healed me of severe migraines, after I was beginning to know Him, I would be lying in bed and more times than I could count, someone would call needing prayer! This was **excellent** quick-acting medicine to free me totally from myself, and since it is a part of my **calling** Eph. 1:18 it was as always the great wisdom of God!

Jesus is "the living bread which came down from heaven," John 6:51 in pure, perfect indisputable humility! However, you surely know Satan is satiated with pride Isa. 14:12-14 and that his evil produces **wormy** bread which discredits, plants doubts, unbelief and filthy lies about Jehovah God at every opportunity, as he tries to slap us down or scare us by doling out **black fear** in increasing doses! I call fear **"black"** because it always brings darkness. Why do you think there are so many people on TV programs, hashing and rehashing in ugly detail the evil he's done, thereby risking building a **memorial** to his wicked antics? This causes **fear** to increase and without Jesus in the picture, **everybody** is totally devoid of answers! Doesn't this keep the door **wide open** for additional nightmares, flashbacks, self-pity, anxiety attacks and slippery pits? These are traps set against healthy growth!

Ephesians 5 warns us about doing this. "11Take no part in *and* have no fellowship with the fruitless deeds *and* enterprises of darkness, but instead [let your lives be so in contrast as to] expose *and* reprove *and* convict them. 12For it is a shame even to speak of *or* mention the things that [such people] practice in secret. 13But when anything is exposed *and* reproved by the light, it is made visible *and* clear; and where everything is visible *and* clear there is light." AMP

The first time or two a traumatic event is discussed with Father God and Jesus and possibly with a mature Christian is one thing, assisting Scripturally in working emotional and mental healings but repeating over, over, over, over and over builds more and more layers on your mountain of pictures, sorrows, fears and more in your mind, becoming a detrimental stronghold. 2 Corinth. 10:4 This grows higher than Mt. Everest and **sends** an invitation to Satan to bomb your mind with questionings, festering wounds in your emotions, welcoming grief spirits, erasing hope, building discouragement and rehashing ad infinitum! Because Satan brought it through the person(s), he will perpetuate and enable you to recall details or fabricate more which should not be told at all!

The Scriptures are very clear regarding traumas of this nature. I'm also reminded of Philippians 4 which clearly tells us what to concentrate on in order to renew and continually progress in acquiring the mind of Christ in us! "6Be anxious for nothing, but in everything by prayer and supplication, with thanksgiving, let your requests be made known to God; 7and the peace of God, which surpasses all understanding, will guard your hearts and minds through Christ Jesus. 8Finally, brethren, whatever things are true, whatever things *are* noble, whatever things *are* just, whatever things *are* pure, whatever things *are* lovely, whatever things *are* of good report, if *there is* any virtue and if *there is* anything praiseworthy — meditate on these things."

We must keep on keeping on remembering that God's Words are for the purest and most joyful, abundant living, James 1:17 while Satan is a **legalist** and doesn't care how he invades your life! He will even regroup his cohorts, if necessary, and come into your life another sneaky way when possible, because his goal is to occupy your body, Matt. 12:43-45 destroy your anointing, discredit and attack God constantly! He and his wicked buddies have deceived the Body of Christ for multitudes of years. They remind me of a pack of rats, which keep gnawing and chewing away in one place and then another and even another, always devious in the **darkest** places!

Beloved Reader, are you now beginning to be enlightened as to why Satan has created a glaring aversion to the Blood, in many ways in the hearts of Christians, even to extremes of eliminating **Blood songs** from hymnals and the **Cross** from churches, which truths are essential to salvation? Some leaders I know, who travel extensively in the USA, have told me these things are happening. We **must** tromp on Satan's head and eradicate his putrid plans. Just a reminder — you are to keep him "under your feet" Rom. 16:20; Luke 10:19 where Jesus has placed him, under "de-feat" of the Body of Christ. Why, because Jesus totally defeated all the heinous powers of darkness. Eph. 1:22 ; Heb. 2:8 Glory to God.

One caution, in Luke 10:19 the correct translation of Jesus' words states, "Behold, I give you the authority to trample on serpents and scorpions, and over all the power of the enemy, and nothing shall by any means hurt you." Consider these truths: **Jesus** is the Speaker, there-fore no argument, as He cannot lie! John 14:6 He made this **powerful** statement to His **un**saved followers, not yet baptized in the Holy Spirit; they **knew** Him and watched Him obtain **complete** victory for over three years in His endeavors with people, displaying many signs and wonders. Later after this, He totally defeated **all** the "principalities, ... powers, ... rulers of the darkness of this age," and "spiritual *hosts* of wickedness in the heavenly *places*," Eph. 6:12 victoriously conquering hell Acts 2:27 KJV and taking the **keys** of death and hell. Acts 2:31 KJV; Revelation 1:18 KJV He took His plunder recorded in Colossians 2:15, "Having disarmed principalities and powers, He made a public spectacle of them, triumphing over them in it." In the *Linguistic Key to the Greek New Testament pg 575* by Fritz Rienecker/Cleon Rogers the meaning of the word **triumph** in Greek means "to lead in a triumph. It pictures a victorious general leading his prisoners in a triumphal procession."

Now Jesus is **active** as our High Priest, as well as being our Lord. Wuest reveals Jesus needed to take His Blood to the heavenlies, going through Satan's domain in order to complete the work of the atonement of the Old Covenant high priest, when he sprinkled the animals' blood on the mercy seat in the Holy of holies! This is taken from *Wuest's Word Studies in the Greek New Testament, Volume 1, The Exegesis of Colossians. pg 209* Isn't it exciting to understand as Almighty God brings the mysteries of puzzlement from the Old Testament into the New Testament reality?! SELAH!

# CHAPTER 4

# Your Faith Glasses Have Zoom Lenses

Often I hear and see covenant children of Jehovah God asking for things **already** provided in the **Better Covenant** beautifully revealed in Hebrews and elsewhere in the New Testament! We truly need to apply our **faith glasses** and **faith hearing aids,** remembering we can **know** and **have** the mind of Christ, consequently realizing more closely how God does love, act and think. We need to understand we are one, **united** with Christ and are **already** seated positionally in the throne room. Eph. 2:6 In fact Almighty God will share His heart many times, when we can be trusted in obedience, if we hunger to love Him, to learn to **wholly trust** Him and understand Him and His **ways!** Matt. 6:33 AMP

Ethel, who discipled me, said her husband called her a "basket weaver!" Really that is brilliant, because of the advantages in seeing the prophetic connection of the Old interlaced into the New Testament, realizing every word and happening have present reasons and future revelations in and from God. For example in Exodus 12, giving **explicit** directions to His Chosen people for their First Passover, God had to pass judgment on the Egyptians because of their oppression of the Israelites, so they were to prepare a perfect male lamb to eat, pointing to our Lamb of God, Jesus, to be sacrificed. They were to "7take *some* of the blood and put *it* on the two doorposts and on the lintel of the houses where they eat it."

Here is a picture of the Cross, on which Jesus would be crucified. The blood of animals protecting **then,** but the **Blood** of our Lord Jesus, the Lamb of God, would be **perfect** protection **daily** from death and destruction after He delivered It unto God. Why was protection required then? You may recall because God had to send the death angel to "12strike all the firstborn in the land of Egypt, both man and beast; and against all the gods of Egypt I will execute judgment: I *am* the Lord. 13Now the blood shall be a sign for you on the houses where you *are.* And when I see the blood, I will pass over you; and the plague shall not be on you to destroy *you* when I strike the land of Egypt." Exod. 12

Dear Reader, if you recall the plagues, representing the **ten false** gods the Egyptians worshipped, you will perceive God was **trying** to awaken the pharaoh and the people to **repent** and **change.** God is a Good, Giving God James 1:17 but He created this world Genesis 1 and has the **exclusive** right to demand willing obedience **best for us.** Please do **not mix your seed** of the Word, by blaming God for evil and crediting Satan with good. See John 10:10.

Also, did you know that lambs, when being slaughtered, look right in the eyes of the person performing the action? They are meek and do not struggle but look face to face. Thus our **perfect Lamb** of **God** reveals limitless attributes in His willingness to obey His Father, though perfect, taking the sins of every person ever born, **never** committing sin Himself but still forgiving each and every one of us!

In our covenant we should **persistently** recall the accomplishments of Christ for each of us on the old rugged Cross, remembering in the covenants in the Old Testament they could only look forward seeing mere types and shadows of what the **Better Covenant** in the **Blood** of **Jesus** would accomplish! Luke 22:20; Heb. 8:6 The leaders in the Old Testament did look forward to the future **hopefully** for what was to come, however. Heb. 11:13 But in all relationships, knowing the extent of the **Better Covenant** is of supreme importance, for we are able then to discern what Jesus accomplished on the **Cross,** what He has done and is doing today right now on earth, as Lord, High Priest and Perfect Intercessor for His Body, even when He comes **again** as **King** of kings to take His believers to Heaven!

Many of our actions have covenant meanings, which when we're aware of them, they increase and deepen our appreciation and understanding of covenant. Many in the Western world lack significant understanding of covenant and the depth of meaning, therefore are deficient in experience, which can result in disrespect in numerous areas of living. For instance, marriages themselves are vitally important to God for He is the Third Person in the marriage. Some signs of the covenant are wedding rings, vows, handshakes, integral partnerships in business, a heart desire to give continually to close friends and others and to honor one another with a toast at a gathering. God loves us so much He even exchanges our name. For example, He renamed Abram to Abr**ah**am and Sarai to Sar**ah.** Gen. 17:5, 15 God built in part of His Name, originating with Jehov**ah.** Your covenant name after Christ and His anointing is what? It is **Christ**ian — how honored can we be? Exchanging names is part of being in covenant.

However, we do need **rhema** understanding that Satan is fearful of the anointing, authority and dynamic power of God's Word in us, when we realize, really believe and act on it in faith. Just for full understanding in the **Bible,** the words "believes in" have much depth and coverage, for "believes in" means "trusts, clings to, relies on." John 3:16 AMP We as believers are to **believe in Jesus Christ!** It is very necessary to recognize when we are **believing in** our **minds only,** which is mental assent, versus actually **believing in our hearts,** which is **faith!** Therefore knowing the whole meaning should help you realize when you are in mental assent rather than **faith.**

A **logos** word is, explaining it simply, when God has **spoken** something and you receive it! The Holy Bible is really the **logos,** Jesus could be called the **Logos,** the will of God and His **promises.** But a **rhema** word is something God has said, upon which you have meditated in faith, tasted, planted to grow in your heart, and is real, **alive** in your spirit and you **know** it, so you **meaningfully apply** it in your own experience in daily living. Because of all the revelation and because Jesus is the Word made flesh, John 1:1, 14 He also could be called the **Rhema,** I think. Yippee!

For example in James 4:7, if you obey in submitting to God and resisting the enemy, you believe the devil flees from the **authority** of **God** and His Word in you! But we cannot take the word "submit" lightly, because every word counts. I try to remind myself when reading James, he was the brother to Jesus both physically and spiritually, so I listen even more attentively! Also, "submit" is a military term and therefore, you "align yourself under" our God. Glory to God. Do you now see why it is so **vital** to **stay** in and **speak** the Written Word? You have riches in abundance for your spirit, soul and body, as the Holy Spirit reminds you!

Without the **Love** of **God** sending His Son to the **Cross** and the heart **decision** by Jesus to come to earth, costing Him an **unfathomable** price every second of every day, you and I would have **no fellowship** restored to God and **no** place to live eternally except in hell. How **utterly tragic** — a place designed for despicable, hideous, heinous, openly rebellious and completely **evil spirits!** Matt. 25:41 Yet, some created beings to whom God gave free will to make choices, **decide** through confusion, perhaps doubt, unbelief in God, lack of understanding or pride, resulting in deception and disobedience, to live there **eternally!** John 3:17-18

Can we truly fathom what eternity is? Since this covenant plan was laid down before the foundation of the world Eph. 1:4-6 and perfectly accomplished by Jesus in Whom God was well pleased, Matt. 3:17; John 19:30 why would anyone even imagine **Almighty God** would **want** to send any person to hell? 1 John 4:9-10 Especially when Jesus **chose** to leave Heaven, come to earth where He said and did **only** what Father God ordered. John 14:10 He never sinned, went through **separation** from God, Matt. 27:46 enduring excruciating pain, sorrow and grief, constant criticism and absolute hell! Yet He did **all** to fulfill the **very** precious promises to **every** person born and to be born.

He promised He would live **in you** and **you** would **live in Him** and **in the Heavenly Father,** John 14:20-23; Acts 17:28 and the **Holy Spirit** would come and live in you as well. John 14:16-17; Acts 2:4, 17 He promised He'd prepare a place for you in Heaven John 14:2-3 and many, many, many other wonderful promises are in His Holy Bible. Also, can you understand the **depth** of **hurt** and **immense** sacrifice that **Father God suffered,** when He allowed His Son to **undergo** for each of us such separation, and a **broken** Spirit, Soul and Body when **He had always lived** in **perfect love** and **obedience?**

Dearly Beloved, can **you** comprehend the dastardly, deceptive trickery interspersed by our enemy? If not, why not stop reading and ask God to enlighten you immediately! Perhaps we fail to recognize that what Jesus accomplished on the Cross **was** and is the **highest form** of **love** in God's **plan,** and is the **only way** to restore our relationship with God, John 14:6 shattered totally by Adam! 1 Corinth. 15:21-22 What an act of utter perfection is unveiled by our perfect **God Man.**

Beloved, if you have been to some extent uncertain or confused, why not be honest and ask God to reveal Himself to you pronto? You will immediately be flooded with waves of peace! Spiritually, scales of blindness will drop off your eyes and you will instantly be amazed at the goodness of Jehovah God! Joy and shalom will truly flood your innermost being, your spirit and soul. Wheeeeee! Everything will be new and you'll see through your faith zoom lenses for sure.

**No one else** loves you nor understands you so completely, eternally, unconditionally and with perfection as does Father, Daddy God. John 3:14-17; Rom. 8:15, 31-39 We think mistakenly we fully understand ourselves! Never — only what God reveals to us — for He is the only One who **knows** us totally, revealing only perfect truth, for He perceives us with our potential included, when He is allowed to work with and through us! **He** is Faith.

Occasionally it really does help to remind ourselves that though we **are** a whole new creation, 2 Corinth. 5:17 when we respond and accept Jesus as Lord and Savior, Rom. 10:9-10 we do still have an **unchanged** body of flesh inherited from Adam's fall, as all creation is awaiting the sons of God to be made manifest Rom. 8:19 with a glorified, indestructible body. Phil. 3:20-:21 Our body will not be redeemed until that day comes, either at the Rapture or when we're in Heaven. 1 Corinth. 15:51-57 Therefore, we need to realize **health** is encased within the covenant, not just healing, so we need to guard our bodies and treat them with God's wisdom and understanding for they have been "fearfully and wonderfully made." Psa. 139:14 We need to remove mountains of destruction against our bodies. Stay strongly in **total forgiveness,** too, so no obstacles are left to trip us. Let's slam dunk symptoms as quickly as they hit, decreeing and declaring applicable Scriptures, and take communion to seal our Bible words.

You each have your individual privilege from God to "work out your own salvation with fear and trembling" Phil. 2:12 by **renewing** your minds, so you can "prove what *is* that good and acceptable and perfect will of God." Rom. 12:2 But you may say, "I thought salvation is a gift." Indeed it is, salvation of your spirit and soul, but **you** do **need** to "receive with meekness the implanted word, which is able to save your souls." James 1:21 We are not earning salvation, just responding to **our** part as co-workers with God, so we can mature and be changed into Christ's image. 2 Corinth. 3:18 Dearly Beloved, please **know** we are not playing games with God!

There are surely numerous questions we can have regarding the Blood, **many** of which are now being revealed in these last days! The value of It cannot be measured, but **Peter** was the one given a very, very valuable truth about It when the Holy Spirit through him called It "precious." 1 Pet. 1:19 (How marvelous the Holy Spirit revealed It through Peter!)

I discovered this one day when the Lord directed me to **honor His Blood.** I said, "Lord, I know It's alive and anointed, but is there a Scripture saying this?" God is so gracious, He led me to discover what **precious** meant in the Greek; it means according to *The New Strong's Expanded Exhaustive Concordance of the Bible Red-Letter Edition,* "costly, **honored,** and esteemed!" This elevates and deepens the value in Almighty God's heart as well as in ours, if we believe and allow the Holy Spirit to assist us in comprehension!

So we're off on an adventure to appreciate, understand and realize the vast, incalculable value in applying and utilizing the Blood of Jesus in accompaniment with the Name above every name, "Jesus." Phil. 2:9-11 In fact, over a year ago, Father God told me when **using** the Name of Jesus to include **His Blood.** I capitalize It because It is alive, powerful, speaks, and It is anointed and honored by Our Heavenly Father. Many of the Body of Christ have **not** yet realized "the width and length and depth and height" Eph. 3:18 of the love of Christ and the value of His Blood — **Its immeasurable** worth — but that can change rapidly. In fact, may the Holy Spirit start changing our limited knowledge and understanding now, as He teaches us through walking, skipping, and running onward in this journey.

As you are reading, would you keep in mind constantly that **He** is **The Teacher?** John 14:26 Please take time, if it's a new thought or where your need is, to see the **truth** by finding and praying over Scriptures in the Bible!

1 Thessalonians 5:19-21, AMP "19Do not quench (suppress or subdue) the (Holy) Spirit. 20Do not spurn the gifts *and* utterances of the prophets — do not depreciate prophetic revelations nor despise inspired instruction or exhortation or warning. 21But test *and* prove all things [until you can recognize] what is good; [to that] hold fast."

If for some reason you still can't stand hearing about or seeing blood, I would like to include a Scripture here, which will be planted in your spirit and can be growing and changing your attitude before we discuss it more. Okay? It's Leviticus 17:14, AMP "As for the life of all flesh, the blood of it represents the life of it; therefore I said to the Israelites, 'You shall partake of the blood of no kind of flesh, for the life of all flesh is its blood. Whoever eats of it shall be cut off.' "

These are God's words here. Perhaps with some of you, it is an aversion from some traumatic experience. In that case, the Blood of Jesus can erase the "mind picture" and then replace it with the realization, through the Scripture above, of the reality of the **living Blood** of **Jesus.** Then why not honor your love of Almighty Father and ask Him to change your thinking to agree with Him on the spot! John 14:21 If you meditate on the Scripture above, Beloved, the aversion will disappear and your decision will enhance greatly what you gain and glean from this journey! Furthermore you will bless the heart of God.

Since the Bible establishes the importance of covenant and the blood from Genesis to Revelation, we need to continue growing daily in understanding and to recognize the importance in revealing greater power in God's Words! Remember the **rainbow** is **God's sign** of the **everlasting covenant** between Him, us and the earth! Gen. 9:12-13 In

Heaven there is a **rainbow** around God's throne Rev. 4:3 as a **continual** reminder never to be forgotten. One time God lovingly kept a patch of rainbow in the sky for many miles as John and I drove from Port Townsend to Sequim, Washington. Rarely do you see one lasting that long, but He whispered within, **"I'm doing this as a treat for you, because you are a proclaimer of My Covenant, thereby honoring it."** So you see it is God's sign, not the enemy's!

But now I am going to reveal some of the events in my life so you'll understand how applicable the Scriptures are to daily living, regardless of what generation it is, leading into why I needed the Holy Spirit in greater fullness, and why and how I was led into continuing an ongoing study and application of the Blood in many ways. May this generate and rekindle reasons in your own life to dig into the understanding and revelation more thoroughly to assist your interest, growth in love and successful living Josh. 1:8 for Almighty Jehovah, the Lord Jesus and the Holy Spirit.

# CHAPTER 5

# Formative Years

In my youngest memories, I do not recall when I didn't **love** Jesus for I was taken to Sunday school regularly. Also, perhaps because of a home where my parents truly loved each other, but were ignorant of the **vital** need of living in harmony and almost nothing about avoiding strife, James 3:16 AMP I needed Jesus when very young. Strife of course kept the door wide open for confusion, mental and physical abuse and frequent contention. I can remember calling out to Jesus, sensing I **might** be loved by Him, but surely needing help desperately for I was very limited in my understanding.

In the darkest part of night was when Satan and his helpers too often had their way with my parents with frequent fights and I wondered if they would kill each other. Dad once threw hot coffee on Mom, then called a doctor who, when he came to our home, put a mustard plaster on her. Then Dad angrily flung the doctor out. Her screams filled the house and echoed in my ears for days. Another time there was a knife involved in the argument but not used! God's **amazing** protection! Still another time, we were riding in the car and they were fighting horribly, when Mom was threatening to jump out of the car, but did not.

But now my Daddy God has **healed all** the pain and the past memories. Even as a child, I seemed to sense Jehovah God was somehow intervening to protect each one of us. I'm now certain someone was praying, who knew how to pray, led by the Holy Spirit, a true believer applying the Scriptures, because of such frequent and frantic need. God requires our Holy Spirit **inspired** prayers to be mixed with Bible faith, in order to **intervene** in our lives because He's given us free will and the anointing, power and authority to move mountains! Mark 11:22-25 He completed His work in His Covenant, so we need to declare, decree or prophesy if we lack anything already provided, so our High Priest has "fresh bread" to use. We have an important responsibility.

My Brother, who is five years older, when a little boy had prayed eagerly for a sister. He was my champion as much as possible; he often intervened in these times of strife, while I frequently hid under the bed listening with ear phones to a crystal set (predecessor to the radio) as a partial restriction to the furor. Then my brother would attempt to terminate the fracas!

Mom was extremely sensitive as she was a lady of tender refine-ment but knew not how to throw her cares to God, 1 Pet. 5:7 so emotional hurts were buried in disgrace and shame inside, as worry and anxiety built up. These facts plus heavy physical labor such as shoveling coal into our furnace, washing clothes in a boiler the hard way, and moving heavy furniture to maintain a perfectly clean home, I believe in time took its toll on her physical body!

You should recognize Dear Readers, that for **many centuries,** myriads of Christians did not understand the "nuts and bolts" of spiritu-ally proceeding by overcoming or getting out of impossible trials and pitfalls, highly desired by **scores** of morally good people! Consequently, they suffered hideous things in secret; hence these things were kept inside and endured. I think the hard work of many people would assist in absorbing their stinging thoughts and pains and were concealed, being buried deeper and deeper, so not healed. I refer to this as **emotional cancer,** which today if we're willing to be **vulnerable,** we can attack in faith, utilizing Scriptural ways through principles of God, great power in the Word, the powerful Name of Jesus and His Blood!

Also, when I was a child, **divorces** were humiliating, made into gossip events and were most undesirable socially as an answer! Things were kept undercover as **dishonorable** secrets. At eleven or twelve years old, when my parents got divorced, I was certain it would be on the front page of the newspaper and everyone would read it. Of course it was not. We are so **blessed** to live **now,** when we have so much revelation in the Scriptures and the "know-how" to apply them in anointing, power and authority, for those who desire to have their "outward expressions changed into the same image from one degree of glory to another according as this change of expression proceeds from the Lord, the Spirit, this outward expression coming from and being truly representative of our Lord." 2 Corinth. 3:18 Wuest. Those who know marriages are covenants with Father God Malachi 2.14-16 deeply **desire** unbreakable ones! Father God, Jesus, Holy Spirit — the Three in One — plus male husband and female wife! "A threefold cord is not quickly broken." Ecclesiastes 4:12

On the **funtastic** side though I was blessed in many ways. Our schools and God's seasons gave us much. In junior high our home rooms gathered leaves in the fall, energetically competing for a prize. At home we had jumping feats into huge leaf heaps, bonfires, wiener and marshmallow roasts salted with campfire songs and stories. In winter in grade school, we had toboggan rides into the sunken sports field, snow igloos with mounds of snowballs for contests and at home we went sledding many places and ice skating on a frozen pond in a park about a mile away for free! Sometimes there were rides on bobsleds being pulled by a truck all around the park. I don't remember school ever being cancelled because of weather!

We had plenty of exercise because our grade and high schools were about a half mile away, while junior high was over one mile. We walked to and from, in fact I have never ridden a school bus! In spring there were many outdoor games at school and even more at home — roller skating, chalk games, jacks, "kick the can," jump rope, hide 'n seek and more. At junior high May was very special because we had a Maypole, and a May fete with many competitive games — throwing the discus, distance and high jumping, running, and on and on. In our neighborhood all ages of children played games together for there were no gangs, so no gang wars. Our God totally balanced the scales again!

Back then a personal relationship with Jesus was not as deeply enjoyed by as **many** Christians as today either! In addition it may be difficult to fathom but the jobs for women were miniscule, so escaping an ugly situation for a woman was not as common as today. There were no refuge places to hide, be helped or escape to, for moral living was the way more people chose to live! When shelters were needed, discerning families helped, as did my Aunt Louise; she gave room and board to a single, pregnant woman, hiring her to help with housework and child care, and never referring to what had happened. **Many** have not known that Jesus **took** our disgrace on the **Cross** by being naked and stripped of all privacy and abused so dishonorably and despicably.

Never did **any** neighbor befriend us during our **frightfully** dark episodes and I think probably Mom and I may have blamed ourselves often for different reasons, as possible instigators, setting Dad's anger off, but each of us is responsible in Christ for our own attitudes and reactions to others! I know the enemy and his tribe are always in the background, wherever they can penetrate and drive a wedge into relationships in God's family. In fact when I was in church in the late 1980s, in the spirit I saw a preen hammer with a sharp, many-sided spike midway on the head. God explained, **"This is what the enemy wants**

**to hit relationships with to weaken them, keeping at it with both ends of the hammer and then using the spike to separate the relationships, especially in marriages and families."** How? Obviously they work through lying words whispered and spoken, actions done destructively.

In the church we attended then there was **no true** understanding or belief regarding Satan and his gruesome ways. I was in a Bible class of about ten couples in a main denomination and I was the only person, other than the teacher, who thought Satan was **real** and a fallen angel! What were we doing with our Bibles in those days? Many of us must have read them not as a **living** book, but more like an **ordinary** secular book or ancient history book, or on Sunday hearing about events happening eons ago, and not at all applicable today. Perhaps some regarded the Bible as mythical or fiction, and many of us definitely read it minus the Holy Spirit's revelation and teaching, treating it as a historically **dead** book. **Nothing** could be **farther** from the truth! Today thank God for **His Light** and many **revelations,** exposing the enemy's lies constantly and for the many ministries reaching out in scores of ways in the United States and the world.

In fact, I recall after I was Holy Spirit baptized, having been led to a different church where I led the prayer group, there was a sweet ninety-year old lady who fell asleep sometimes. I would quickly pray and off her lap would go her Bible and wake her; almost always she'd be praying in tongues as she awoke. I truly believe it was God's sense of humor, revealing His Living Word and the presence of the Holy Spirit. My own understanding and knowledge of the Bible was also greatly enlarged, **overhauled, changed,** sometimes **renewed,** and **refreshed** positively almost from the instant that I received the Holy Spirit Baptism! What a **revolutionary** effect it had and still does in my prayer life and daily living. Amazing! (Though not 90 years old yet, I do have a faithful female Dalmatian dog who wakes me if I doze off on some occasions or naps with me.)

As for our family, Dad was on the road a great deal during the week, and was possibly dishonorable in his actions regarding the marriage covenant. At any rate, because of demonic activity and his emotional behavior, we never knew **what** would anger him greatly when he came home, because in much of his behavior he was led by his emotions and feelings! He had a tender and humorous side, which was revealed more often when others were present than at home when alone with us. I think he probably helped care for the younger six children in his family as he grew up, and became habitually bossy, which resulted in taking charge in a domineering way as a habit, rather than leading in a Christ-like loving way in the marriage. In fact, he was probably a very merciful person, according to the so-called "motivational" gifts from God Rom. 12:6-8 but in much pollution. (His Father was a preacher in country churches until he was over 90!) He and Mom tried to get through very tough times, especially financially, and specifically when his secretary, not bonded, stole **many** thousands of dollars from the insurance company for which he worked! Dad stayed with that company, paying back slowly **every cent** she stole!

When we had visitors, Dad could impress a mouse with his charm and sense of humor! As I grew older he would show off my strength by having me lift him up and he would show how big my feet were by putting his feet in my shoes. One incident of far greater seriousness involving me gave Mother courage to get a divorce, when I was in junior high school, and I blamed myself secretly but it was not my fault. This was revealed to me by a word of knowledge 1 Corinth. 12:8 in a one day Spirit-filled class seminar I attended a number of years after I was married.

Mom was very sensitive, feminine, practical, immensely creative and made many things, sewing like a professional; she even made her own maternity clothes, dad's shirts, costumes for dance recitals, doll clothes, later even size four suit pants for my son, et cetera! What a homemaker she was! She wisely investigated eating properly, **uncommon** when she was a housewife, by subscribing to a Boston magazine on cooking, which was advanced for that time, revealing proper foods to eat — fruits, vegetables and meats, in very well-balanced portions with much variety.

I can recall picking dandelion leaves for greens to eat, **yet** lack was **never spoken** aloud thanks to the wisdom of God in Mom. I doubt if she knew the abundant Scriptures regarding the tongue and our usage to prevent damages, but in raising us she was surely **guarded,** even after the divorce. She also did many fun things with me like knitting, crocheting, making valentines, May baskets filled with our home grown flowers, which we secretly left on people's doorknobs on May first and food treats for others. She helped cook meals for church and kept the housework done to perfection. She played the piano by ear and sang like a lark. Yes, she even roller-skated with us in the street around our home.

She also could have been an interior decorator and a professional dress designer due to her God-given abilities and ideas with impeccable taste — to know what belonged in any home and at a glance what would look best on any individual! When she later worked in a dress shop in California, Catherine Marshall, the authoress, would purchase dresses and Mom knew precisely what she would like. She also literally saved the life of a pilot, who crashed on the open fields of my Uncle's large estate in Palatine, Illinois. She received a personal letter of commendation from the President of the United States at the time.

When we're "born again" John 3:3 into God's family we become new creatures inside **first.** But there are **precious** anointings, I believe given in the womb, some latent or undeveloped talents, as well as pure motivational gifts, given by Jehovah God, Rom. 12:6-8 which are polluted until purified by Him. There are other gifts, actually persons given by Jesus, who are to **equip** and **edify** the saints in the Body of Christ for ministry. Eph. 4:11-16 Father God will initiate these at His discretion, for He designed us individually, and if accepted and fulfilled by someone, He often develops and maintains the growth and promotion of the gift(s) and talent(s) through inheritance from one's biological parents. It seems particularly true in these days when strong Christians have been in the lineage of a family for several generations and have assisted others in diverse facets of the ministry of Jesus! **Each** person born on this earth is needed and has an individual **calling** from God to fulfill God's plan for his life and be born into the large family He desires! Eph. 1:17-18

Do I hear some of you saying, "However He surely does not need me!" Well, would you please consider this seriously, if His Creativity is so **spacious** that there are never any two snowflakes alike, why would He do **less** with **individuals** made in His image? Gen. 1:27

# CHAPTER 6

## Abba Father's Scales Are Perfectly Balanced

"We love Him" though "because He first loved us!" 1 John 4:19 But Abba Father has **always** "balanced the scales" with "righteousness and justice" in my life, Psa. 89:14 versus unrighteousness and injustice. Sad circumstances with joyful events developed a stronger **trust** in Him which has amplified my love, and increased my spiritual and mental stability. I even own a **scales** of **justice** to keep me aware at all times of His perfect Judgment and Blessings, which He continually pours out. (Our daughter even at two years old asked us to sing *"Count Your B'essings,"* which we surely did, for here in our arms was **one** blessing, buried in my heart for fourteen years.)

However my fickle emotions, hurtful feelings and undesirable incidents were not released and yielded to the Holy Spirit's control until many years later, when I learned to be led by the Holy Spirit. Nevertheless, Father God protected our family and me in so many countless ways, that I know our family must have kept the intercessors very busy, for nothing magnificent enters the visible world unless someone **prays.** Never can I **thank** Almighty God enough for His goodness, love, patience and faithfulness!

God provided "escapes" with friends, where I could have freedom emotionally and good clean fun away from home at times when my parents were together, as well as after the divorce. When I was young, we had a neighbor girl whose family permitted us to play often in their yard, for her father had built a small railroad station with a passenger car to ride a brief way uphill. At the end of the ride was a small waiting station, from where we'd slide into a small round pool, which we often sat around, played games and splashed. Another family had an older son, an amazing wood carver, who could create almost anything! For example he would form a linked chain from one piece of wood and carve all kinds of animals; I'd watch him by the hour. Another family in the neighborhood practically accepted me as a second daughter. There'll be more about them later.

In junior high school I had a music teacher who was very good to me, as a friend. I also had a treasured Jewish friend my age, who was sharp mentally and very humorous; we would have such fun and I'd laugh so hard I'd often get in trouble during class, being told more self-control was in order for me. The friendship was ended abruptly when we graduated to high school, because her mother did not want her to have a Gentile friend! This was difficult, because I so enjoyed her and she did maintain an adult Gentile teacher as a close friend. She became an actress in live theater and movies though, and a few years ago I did get a glimpse of her on a movie screen, as she was one of the nuns in the *Sister Act.*

Mother's parents were very good to me, and maintained a peaceful and loving home. They were also openly respectful and deeply in love with one another, until Grandmother Ruhl graduated to Heaven at age 79. Later I realized they were my example of God's shining **love covenant** as I grew up; sometimes on week-ends I was allowed to go to their home by street cars or walk. Occasionally, I was even allowed to stay all night. They had an immense home with 3 fireplaces — a library room, a solarium, a parlor, dining room, living room, seven bedrooms, a glass enclosed sleeping porch, a huge kitchen with an enormous pantry, and two sinks — one with well water. They also had a huge attic with superb hiding places and enough empty floor space to ride tricycles, even roller-skate! I was even allowed to slide down the banister two stories long — just for fun. They also had a barn garage. We were taught to respect possessions and use them, not keep them untouchable.

Other times I was allowed to sleep in the large bedroom with the huge upstairs fireplace, where all their children had been born. At night as I went to sleep, I was delighted to watch shadows dancing on the ceiling, when a few cars went by. Also upstairs sometimes in winter I slept in the unheated, glassed-in porch balcony, just to enjoy the cold. Remember Beloved, we had no TV, few movies in theaters only and no common stereo equipment, very few cars, so our world was **much simpler** and **quieter!** Their home was made into a large apartment when my grandparents graduated to Heaven.

One of my Great Aunts lived in a lovely home in Illinois, where each room was furnished in a different wood such as cherry, oak, mahogany, walnut and others. She owned a summer place where I had such fun playing in a near-by creek with her Collie. My Grandfather Ruhl built a summer cottage in Clear Lake, Iowa. It had a ladder going upstairs from the kitchen but a stairway in the living room. He used a huge boiler outdoors as a water heater on a pole, using solar energy. What fun we had! He **built** Mom and Dad's home, too, **given** to them as a wedding present! It was still being lived in and was as pretty as could be, just a decade ago. He attended school only through the eighth grade, fathered seven children, and paid for the five living children to attend college. He loved to listen to classical music artists such as Amelita Galli-curci, Enrico Caruso, Lily Pons and others on the radio or on Edison's thick records, played on an old RCA Victrola. The Victrola was the forerunner to long-playing records in stereos.

51

Grandma would make up stories to tell me and was a super cook, her specialty was raised doughnuts! She would allow me to experiment with cooking in her enormous kitchen. Once she let me make fudge, which was very runny, so I took it home on the streetcar, hid it under our house to cook it again later to surprise Mom. I was the one surprised because I failed to count on so many creepy things liking it, too! Other times I played in the barn, where Grandfather later had his pet talking rooster to keep him company, when he worked out there on his various projects. He wrote a beautiful letter to me on maturing, when I turned thirteen. He worked until he was eighty-eight at his office, located in downtown quite a distance from his home. We sometimes played dominoes or cards. We would also often sit on the long front porch, watching and visiting with people walking by, and with the vegetable man and the ice man (for ice **boxes** in those days were used to keep perishable edible items). On warm days the kids were allowed to eat ice chips and pet the horses pulling their carts! What a delight that was!

One interesting event when I was in earlier grade school, perhaps a sign of the times, was a field trip. The two exciting (?) places chosen were to the Polk County Poor Farm and to the insane asylum! I can still remember one poor lady in a rocking chair with the saddest eyes and muttering very strange sounds. In later years it has been my heart's desire to help release the mentally sick from captivity! Some demonic deliverances I've been a part of have certainly destroyed many yokes and lifted bondages, Isa. 10:27 but I deeply desire to do much more to assist in making people **whole.** You probably remember in Luke 17 the event on earth when Jesus healed the ten lepers, **only one** returned after being healed, "15and with a loud voice glorified God, 16and fell down on *his* face at His feet, giving Him thanks. And he was a Samaritan." Jesus asked about the **nine** to those around Him, "19And He said to him, 'Arise, go your way. Your faith has made you well.' " "Well" here means **whole.** This portion of Scripture is so pregnant with meaning I could preach were there time and room, so do invite the Holy Spirit to reveal more and more, would you?

Growing up, we children were blessed, indeed, because of all the free fun outdoor activities we could do! As I said, in winter we had ponds in public parks for ice skating and even bobsleds hitched onto cars and at school we had enough hills for toboggans during recess, plus blocked off streets for sleds after school! Then in spring, summer and fall we could bike, swim in inexpensive near-by outdoor pools and go roller-skating, as well. Also, we were in neighborhoods where we truly played with all ages; we had many outdoor activities such as jump rope, hopscotch, "olly olly oxen free," marbles and climbing trees. We had near-by apple and grape orchards, where we were told to eat whenever we chose. We even attended a near-by movie theater for **ten cents** on Saturday mornings! We saw serials, often Westerns, with short episodes but the wicked people were punished and the **good** always were the victors. I even sold my own homemade lemonade and flowers grown in our yard in front of our house, while my brother sold vegetables from door to door. We walked to our schools, as I mentioned earlier, and wherever else we went, even downtown which was three and one-half miles each way, unless we earned enough carfare for one way.

Since my youth, music has been deeply and continually an integral part of me from listening to my mother and brother play the piano, by ear and by reading notes, to my playing easy chords and singing in church choirs, chorus groups, trios and solos in schools; and often times in the Spirit in various Christian meetings and gatherings, on occasion as I was teaching the Word! In high school we sang many hymns and even in combined choirs from all over the state of Iowa. I was in a trio at graduation from high school and for a Christmas program I was an angel (only once) as I perched on a high stool singing the annunciation of the Birth of Jesus with no accompaniment! Now that was a **high** point in my life, for sure.

Even during those years God gave me married couples as friends and I sensed God urging me to be water baptized in Dad's church, in which I grew up, even though my parents were divorced at that time. Years later, as an adult Jesus asked me to be baptized again, because He had become my **Lord!** I had a friend tell me I would go to hell for doing it again! But I remembered Naaman being told to "Go and wash in the Jordan seven times," 2 Kings 5:10 thus decided if pride could be involved, I had **better** do it for sure! He has never let go of me! Amazing, indeed!

# CHAPTER 7

# My Refuge, Fortress, Shield and Buckler

Throughout my life I've been through many experiences where the protection of Father God has been **extraordinary!** In my early childhood I was unaware of the imperishable significance regarding any Scriptures, let alone Psalm 91. However now after much revelation pertaining to an extensive quantity of the Word, and the many facets of it which I've experienced, I must stop to testify, singing unending praises to its **Truth** and **Power.** The **living** Word and the **written** Word are my life line.

This of course **expands** my faith in every direction, because I can **plant stakes** of faith many places, when I remember what God has done so **graciously!** Planting faith stakes can keep your faith and mind perking, when trials and hardships **look** impossible to be solved and you can prayerfully keep it growing! "With God all things are possible!" Matt. 19:26 You see, we can have those stakes labeled to **recall** what God did by decreeing every **victory** stake already established, then with our zoom lens faith glasses look **forward** with "rapid grow" faith, knowing He will solve it again His way **if** allowed. May these true incidents ring a bell, refresh, encourage your own faith and establish new appreciation as your faith enhances **your trust** in our Father and His Word!

Are you familiar with the fairly recent song *He'll Do It Again?* The gist is **if** God did an amazing thing once for you, He will **not** stop because **He** is Faithful, so He will surely do it again; maybe in a different way, because He is so awesome and has multitudes of ideas, but He will bring you through and *"never leave you nor forsake you."* Heb. 13:5

When my brother and I were around 12 and 7 years old, our family headed to our Aunt Louise's home a few days before Christmas. Dad really loved my Aunt Louise, so we piled into our old car with no working heater to drive to Galena, Illinois, during an unusually, dreadfully icy cold, blustery snowstorm. It was so freezing cold, Mother had to pour salt on the outside of the driver's window frequently to keep the ice from totally blocking Dad's vision for the entire trip. We should have arrived in about **six** hours then, but it was so hazardous it took over **fourteen.** However, about thirteen miles before we arrived there safely, an incident almost cost our lives! As we were crossing a very slippery and treacherous bridge, at least that day, from Dubuque, Iowa to Dubuque, Illinois, at the end of the bridge we had to make a sharp right turn, however, suddenly instead the car **slid** a hard **left** hitting a **flimsy** wooden barrier! This barely brought us to a stop, keeping us from careening down hundreds of feet below.

But **God** restrained the car, and protected it and us so we could continue on to Galena **gratefully,** finally landing at Uncle Jack and Aunt Louise's wonderfully cozy, warm and loving home. The angels of Almighty God must have been intervening for our **astonishing** protection. In a family or separate lives, where God is honored, I have seen God repeatedly **prevent tragic** events with His **mighty** shelter. Surely we are under the light we're under at given seasons of our lives and we know people are praying so God **can** act and accomplish miracles. **Lack** of prayer or praying **amiss can** halt His ability to perform what He wishes many times. Consequently we consistently listen to the Holy Spirit.

One day Dad was driving me to my junior high school on his way to meet a client, when we hit a car, probably a 1936 Ford with two doors, and flipped it over. The driver walked out unhurt, so Dad sent me on foot the rest of the way to school. Another incident occurred when I was age twelve, I was swimming at a lake with my girl friend, trying to learn to dive backward off a raft, when I scraped my back because I was too close. I flipped backward under the raft which floated about three inches above the surface of the water, except around the perimeter. Somehow I gasped a little and inhaled quickly enough, swam down under and up to the surface, then onto the raft. At an early age Mother had made certain I'd taken a few swimming lessons from a Hawaiian man. Praise the Lord. Abba God saved me even from fear!

One summer after teaching two years, I was offered a ride home by friends driving to Pennsylvania, who were to drop me off at an Iowa town, where Dad would meet me, driving on to Des Moines. We were on a straight country two-lane road in Iowa, when an older man way down the road from us was acting very indecisively. As he approached his stop sign on a side road, he slowed down, then sped up several times and then drove right in front of us as we came to the intersection! So we smacked him broadside! This was a time when there were few lawsuits and very integral insurance companies; so since he **wasn't hurt,** and we were believed, all was settled easily. What an incredible defense by God!

Another very dramatic intervention by God and His mighty protection was on a nippy wintry evening, when a number of us single teachers were eating at a restaurant on a very high hill in Portland, Oregon. I had only **just** learned to drive **that** summer, because Mom and I did not have a car after the divorce, when I still lived at home. (I'd gone to college, moved to Washington where I walked, or rode a bus until I bought a bicycle.) Later Mom moved to Washington, also, where we lived together, so I occasionally used her car, as I did this particular night, but I had only had my driver's license for five months. As we continued eating, the weather outside was worsening, unknown to us, turning into a black ice storm.

I was going to meet John, my fiancé then, at a designated place, while the rest of the teachers were headed to our high school students' football game near-by! Being **totally** inexperienced on **any** ice, I requested that someone else drive Mom's car, but **all** declined immediately and positively! One **brave** Catholic said he'd ride with me to assist in following the male teacher, who was leading me where I was to meet John. The leader was an experienced driver and was several car lengths ahead of me, when we came to a heavily-coated black top, totally icy bridge! He was crossing at an acceptable speed safely, but I was slowly creeping along, when zigzagging towards me came a car, swerving right into my lane. Of course I applied the brakes — a **"no no"** when on ice — declaring most convincingly with authority, "This is it!" This triggered my male friend into saying what he called his "last rites." Thereupon we hit a concrete curb, spun around about three hundred degrees, rapidly and dramatically, but were stopped most abruptly by it, after I smashed the front end and blew three tires too successfully. But **we** were unhurt! Father God, the Holy Spirit, the Blood of Jesus and His angels were at work!

The ones ahead of us saw the event and came to rescue us, deciding we should still go to the game; I had my Dalmatian dog with me, but we carried on. The game, played in ice and light snow, was a fiasco and the trip back on the bus to Kelso, normally requiring one hour on the road, took over **four!** This was **before** cell phones and it was so treacherous we were permitted to escape the scene, leaving the car which was going nowhere, but not without God's **precious** protection going into action! Glory to God!

Years later, I was driving down a small hill with my friend, Marilyn, when I hit a small patch of ice, zigzagging back and forth, ramming an island of bricks and plantings, also damaging a heavy fence, which protected drivers from going down a cliff several hundred feet. Next, I whacked a tree, planted just prior to a place of business on the right! Thanks be to Almighty Jehovah because I could have smashed into the business, striking several people! God revealed I had totaled my car, contrary to what the policeman and the driver of the tow truck said.

I was also discipling Marilyn at this time, but this surely was not a recommended incident. However for me it became a Victorious Faith Spot for a **stake** indeed, because of God's **protection** again and the fence remains damaged as a reminder even today! However, Marilyn was affected differently, for **fear** clouded her emotions. Some weeks later in a vision I saw **fear** as a red carpet rolling fast like a scroll and hitting her chest. God immediately said, **"She's rolling the red carpet out for the enemy. She needs to roll the red carpet out for Me!"** She realized she'd been focusing on the enemy's lies instead of on what God had done for us.

Soon after I was baptized in the Holy Spirit, I walked through a department store where I spotted a cuckoo clock with two active little dancing figures, playing two different German tunes on the hour and the half hour. I asked the price, since it was not running and was marked $65. The employee said he'd ask his boss when he returned. I noticed it was from the Black Forest in Germany, so I thought it probably would be an easy fix, but I could only afford $20 as I told God. When I called back from home, the manager said I could have it for $25, but I told the employee, "Thank you, but I can only spend $20!" He said quickly, "Wait a minute, **don't** hang up." When he came back, his boss had agreed with my price! God had worked it out for I was not intending to **manipulate** the situation at all. Alleluia! On the way home, I asked a jeweler to examine it, who thought it was fine. John later looked it over and made several minor adjustments and I now had a long-awaited cuckoo clock with **two** songs! Another **faith stake!**

Through the years over all the lives of my family, I've learned to break the **frequency** of automobile **accidents,** particularly because of my Dad's in the past, mine and my son's! I know who's behind them! One Mother's Day after church, a woman told me my son had just been in a car accident and before I reached the scene, Father God said quietly, **"Don't you know the enemy is trying to kill John?"** Another opportunity for Psalm 91, not accentuating the problem!

How do we head Satan off at the pass? By making sure "we are not ignorant of his devices." 2 Corinth. 2:11 In faith **preventing** as many wicked attacks and plans when I **declare** the Blood on vehicles of transportation on the ground, in the air or on the water for others and our family — from tricycles to skate boards, motor bikes to vans, from parachutes to airplanes, and water skis to cruise ships! I **declare** and **decree** the victory of the Blood and accompanying angels over all situations, **prior** to driving, riding or flying anywhere. I have trained my family and others to do likewise.

I pay close attention to each "stop sign" or "check in my spirit" for myself, so I will be in the right place at the right time **always!** I **plead** and **declare aloud** that the Blood is over my pathway, going before me, over my vehicle, as I ask God for His wisdom to drive both **defensively** and **alertly.** When **actually driving** if someone is behind or passing me driving extra speedily, I bind demonic actions, influence and carelessness. I do realize some of these accidents could have been repetitive due to careless driving habits, so I've asked God to reveal where I need to change. One time I had a very minor accident because a car was caught in the middle of an intersection. I barely tapped it and was not given a ticket. However, Almighty God told **me, "You are never to be at all aggressive at any intersection!"** The only way to be on the King's Highway!

# CHAPTER 8

# Psalm 91 ... Reality Revealed

During our years of marriage, now over fifty, I've been spared three head-on collisions, always when I was alone doing the driving; one was on a two-lane road in pouring down rain when the oncoming car had no lights turned on! Another happened on a pretty sunny afternoon recently, on a scenic back road, again only two lanes, when the driver from about two blocks away was driving straight towards me, both of which I saw and was able to avoid, thanks be to God!

The third close call was unknown to me and the Holy Spirit directed, almost audibly, on a steep uphill four-lane road, **"Move over now to the outside lane!"** Whereupon downhill came a truck **pronto,** going somewhat over the speed limit in the lane I had just barely vacated, missing what could have been disastrous for both or either of us! Almighty God keeps us protected always if we are listening **alertly** and obeying the law at all times.

The fourth opportunity for a head-on crash was when a college professor in Oregon was taking me to a bus station and she unknowingly went the **wrong** way on a freeway exit road! This was several years before I was married and again quite an experience. In these days, when others and I are driving, I listen especially for checks in my spirit as a **preventive** measure, making declarations and decrees when I hear or see potential things, quickly applying Scriptures in God's wisdom, **not** in fear but surely in **defensive** and **preventive** faith in action! I've mentioned this more than once on purpose for the sake of you and your families, because **we** are to work the Word and His Written Word works **always!**

When I'm preparing to drive, even before I leave my driveway, because of **vital** importance, I declare and decree the following statements: "I'm **alert** in the Lord Jesus, driving with His wisdom defensively, accompanied by angels, and the Blood of Jesus is covering me, my car — front, back, over and under plus no lumps, bumps, or scratches will occur." I also **loose** safety and I keep listening to the Holy Spirit for roads to take, for I surely have definitely learned that Satan works on preparing possible damaging and destroying set-ups, situations, snares and traps. I also **loudly** declare, "My steps are ordered by the Lord" (Jesus) Psa. 37:23 and I **plead** the Blood, **listening** for any checks in the spirit! John 10:10 speaks volumes of truth regarding the evil planned and performed if possible, by our arch enemy. The Holy Spirit revealed some years ago, if Satan can, he will try stealing in one area, then try killing in the **same** area and try destroying until his wickedness works, if at all possible. **Fear not,** but don't treat him flippantly, for he alone is the killer.

The time spent making these declarations is well worth it. Case in point, I'd been to an appointment one day and was enjoying praying and driving on some picturesque roads on the way home, when I became sleepy. I took authority over my body, as there was no place to pull off the road, and continued on, as I was not far from home. Suddenly, the brakes were **abruptly** applied, which **woke** me, for I had fallen **fast asleep.** My car and I landed in a **pedestrian** crossing at a twelve-lane intersection, after traveling **six-tenths** of a mile on a curving, uphill one-way two-lane road with a ditch on my right! (I checked the **victory** distance later.)

As I awoke, I was **very** startled, **amazed** and puzzled, but to my left was a policeman, awaiting a light change. He approached on foot outside my passenger's window very shortly but where was his car? He asked "How are you, did you black out?" I told him I fell asleep. "Are you sure you are all right and you did not black out?" Then he said "Okay, which way do you want to go? I'll stop the traffic." I asked "Is my car drivable?" He said it was, so I took off, thanking God constantly all the way home, where I soon discovered, there was not a scratch on my car!

Later, when I was going to write a thank you note to the Police Department, I was checked in my spirit, so I decided he must have been an angel, because I was treated so quickly and courteously with no paper reports. Satan may make many vicious plans but God outshines and overrides him every time for sure, contingent upon our obedience and acute listening when we truly know Him! Psalm 91 is a **strong, all** inclusive basic declaration against evil and illnesses said out of my mouth at least once daily.

Another time, I'd been shopping for Sunday school supplies, when I decided to try one more store. Now I heard **very** softly inside, **"Go home,"** but I **stubbornly** went on. I was trying to make a left turn onto a four-lane road, when this van came with its signal light turned on to make a right turn into the parking lot that I was exiting, but he did not. He struck me pretty hard; turned out he was a new driver, but the policeman ruled pronto in **his** favor and I got a ticket, which I knew I was to accept with no argument. He may have left the turn signal on inadvertently but I believe I would have been aware of this in the spirit if I were following **God's** orders!

For years now, I repeat again, Psalm 91 is **daily** declared and decreed in my prayers for us and many others for whom I pray! It is such an active, powerful, complete, and comforting **truth** and so greatly appreciated that by applying this specific Scripture in faith and in love, we reap totally such **supernatural** unparalleled results. Then we are awakened to the awesome certainty that this is only one example out of many we are applying rigorously in faith, but we're almost overwhelmed by the potential value and magnitude, as if swallowed by an avalanche!

We can **intercede** for those who are Christians and for those who will become Christians in the armed forces, others in danger and being persecuted, by utilizing Psalm 91 in **countless ways.** The Holy Spirit revealed to me to declare that they will ask for **discerning** what's afoot, how to pray for foul, dangerous events and to learn to trust Father God completely for mighty protection even in the midst of actual combat!

# CHAPTER 9

# Insatiable Hunger

Though happily married to a faithful husband with many admirable qualities and two very precious children, fifteen months apart in age and truly miraculously conceived, as revealed by my pediatrician several years later, I became spiritually **ravenous** in my forties! I needed something **deeper** in my life! Desperate frustration due to **spiritual** starvation is what I call it now and that probably says it all. I had loved Jesus in my childhood, as far back as I remember, having been raised in a Baptist church; my paternal Grandfather whom I dearly loved was a Baptist minister on whose birthday date and month I was born.

I was led by Jesus to be water baptized at eleven years of age, after which I was immediately assigned to teach 2 and 3 year olds in Sunday school. I was not aware at that time, that I should **ask** Jesus to be my **Lord,** as well as my **Savior,** a **vital** error! I was attending the same church I grew up in, even though Mom and Dad were divorced by this time, but some adults in the choir took me to church so I could continue attending and singing!

When attending college, I had made a firm, bold declaration I would **not** become a teacher. Ha! What did I know? Zilch! Incidents even in junior and senior high school should have been a clue. After my twelfth birthday I took innumerable baby sitting jobs for as many as three or four children at a time for ten cents an hour and fifty cents after midnight. During several summers, starting at age fourteen, I had worked in city parks supervising children, teaching or assisting, doing everything from handicrafts to tennis all day, managing children varying from eight to seventeen years old. Also, my English teacher, when I was in the eleventh grade, told me he wanted to recommend me to teach English that summer at Drake University in Des Moines, Iowa where we lived. He had more faith in me than I, for I refused. Still I really did **not see!**

Almighty God pursued with His idea, because I had a blessed friend in junior high, an English and music teacher, unmarried, who encouraged me to go to college almost as if I were her daughter. Her nephew, Bernard, was attending a Methodist College, Cornell in Mt. Vernon, Iowa, which she regarded very highly and where I could assist financially by earning my room and board. She really did **believe** and **encourage** me to go even though Mother could not afford to send me. And honestly I don't recall how my childless Great Aunt Anna, after whom I was named, learned about my desire, although for all four years she paid tuition while I earned the rest. It was an uncertain arrangement every semester, whether I'd be continuing, but God and she graciously saw me through. My dear teacher, Evelyn, washed my clothes because there were no laundromats in those days. Mom sent money and some new clothes when she could, and I made grades which did get me through.

While at Cornell a highlight was participating in singing in the college choir **all** of Handel's *The Messiah* with professional soloists once yearly. What a delight! Had I had the money, I would have majored in music instead of English with my minor in French. However, **Spiritual** seeds were idealistically planted, for we were required to attend chapel weekdays. The chapel stands on a small knoll on campus and many times I would walk by just to hear the magnificent organ being played and filling the entire area with splendor, beauty, joy and glory.

Since I was not reading the Bible regularly my **spiritual** growth was greatly hindered. We surely must learn we **are** a **spirit,** which needs **regular rich** feeding in order to grow in God's faith, wisdom, understanding, counsel, might, knowledge, peace and even joy.Isa. 11:2 Of course Jesus is all these qualities but we develop them through implanting Scriptures, withdrawing them and releasing the fruit of the Holy Spirit! Gal. 5:22-25 Glory to God.

So at the end of my junior year, still absolutely ignorant of His **big picture** ahead, not realizing it was a part of **His Master plan** for me, I yielded to becoming a teacher. Therefore I had to attend two consecutive summer schools, my senior year as well, in order to fulfill the basic educational requirements, though I had credits for the equivalent of almost five years of education. Do you perceive, Beloved, how God arranges at the beginning of our lives, to order our steps resulting in the fulfilling of His glorious plans designed for us? Eph. 2:10

After college graduation in June, through the Cornell College placement agency, I was offered a position in Colorado or Washington State. When you belong to God, yet you're green in judgment and understanding before truly knowing God intimately, your **reasons** can be wacko, but **He will use** them anyway to **plant** you where He truly wants you. Prov. 16:9 AMP I had told my friends it would be Washington, **if** I received an offer, because I loved its beautiful trees, lakes, mountains, scenery, waterfalls, possibility of ocean trips, apples and it would be cooler weather than Iowa and far away! (How deep can one's thought life and plans be?) The **very** next day, following graduation and the end of my second consecutive summer school in August I took off in flight, first time in an airplane! After landing and bussing from Portland, Oregon to Kelso, Washington, it was midnight and no taxis, so I walked with one suitcase to my new residence, a single room in a home for **twenty** dollars a month!

My adventures in public school teaching began with little fanfare but in earnest, for the **first** year I had a total of **seven** classes, several alternates with an average size of **forty-three** pupils! My practice teaching in college had been with students taught one term yearly by inexperienced teachers all their lives, so the requirement for discipline was almost nonexistent! Besides teaching **boys'** and **girls'** health, eighth-grade science and math, I had a number of English classes. It was very demanding to say the least, but because I was only twenty-two years old, I enjoyed my students too much, so I had to learn pronto to tighten the reins. It was surely God's wisdom leading me, for one beginning teacher left, but I didn't recognize how blessed I was until later, when I realized all He had taught me to do.

I had also been trained in English **only,** so **this** teacher was learning constantly as well. Briefly at one point I even directed a children's choir in church. The conditions leveled off in time and I taught just ninth grade English, though I did take extra classes several summers at a branch of Oregon State University, resulting with a certificate for all twelve grades. After several years, I directed two or three plays a year, practicing right after school, so I stayed very busy.

When I began my years in Kelso, it was a logging town with thirty-four taverns, one very old-fashioned general department store and two drug stores. Most of the population, ten to twelve thousand, lived out in the surrounding hills. About my fifth or sixth year, I decided to try another school in Chehalis, a near-by city, where I was offered a tantalizing position. But I dearly appreciated my principal, who urged me to stay, which I did for five more years; he even painted a picture for me, after I made my decision to remain. Still later I was offered an exchange position for one year in Kelso, Scotland, but refused because my Mother had moved to live with me and we were living in a rental home. Decades later, I did travel to Scotland with Lee LaCoss' Light of Life Ministry. For some reason it seemed like home!

I married during the ninth year of teaching and after five years had my two **deeply** desired children, a girl and a boy! Two years later, I insisted on an exploratory operation to discover why there was no third child. At that time, the head of the department of pediatrics in the hospital, where my two very precious children were born, demanded that the obstetrician remove my uterus on the spot during the actual operation, because it was not in good shape! (I still have it.) My doctor would not, because I was in there to have **more** children. The Mighty Hand of God protected me again. In addition, my doctor was **totally** astonished at all my organs inside, because once again severe endometriosis had invaded so completely that adhesions were rampant, twisted and connected to my inner organs and both fallopian tubes were totally closed.

When I was teaching, the summer after my second year I needed an operation for the same thing, because of severe pain monthly. The second time around I wasn't having any pain, so I had no idea of what had happened internally. My doctor went so far as to say that if he had not attended me at both deliveries of our babies, he would have called me a **liar** because of the severity of the innards. I wanted six children but Father God knows best and after these facts, I appreciated Daddy God even more and realized I was through!

Many years later, after being led to James 1:19-20 a **number** of times, "19Therefore, my beloved brethren, let every man be swift to hear, slow to speak, slow to wrath; 20for the wrath of man does not produce the righteousness of God," I realized we **are** definitely accountable for "every idle word." Matt. 12:36 When we say things with a wrong attitude in **faith, particularly** after we are Spirit-filled, we can wreak havoc by being a prophet to our own detriment in life now and in the future. Are you asking why? We **cannot** deny Proverbs 18:21, AMP

"Death and life are in the power of the tongue, and they who indulge it shall eat the fruit of it [for death or life]." As a result I see **much** uncontrolled anger in this End Time in people of all ages, which will produce disastrous results.

Dearly Beloved, the fact is we have been **empowered** and entrusted with **tremendous** authority and power from Jesus. Decades ago and months prior to a miscarriage and **no** more children, I had blurted out strongly words **in anger** to my dear husband, for which I was the only one responsible. The **result** was **I** could **not** have **any more** children. I said it and God answered **my** words, because He honors our gift from Him of a free will and speech! Also He had to obey my words, because **I believed** what I said. "Fling forth" is surely what I did. In Matthew 12 our Lord Jesus said, "35The good man from his inner good treasure flings forth good things, and the evil man out of his inner evil storehouse flings forth evil things. 36But I tell you, on the day of judgment men will have to give account for every idle (inoperative, nonworking) word they speak. 37For by your words you will be justified *and* acquitted, and by your words you will be condemned *and* sentenced." AMP

When the children were ready, we enrolled them in a Christian school, where they would receive an excellent solid foundation in the **Bible** — spirit, soul and body — and would be taught reinforcing morality and Christian principles, laws and statutes, very basic subjects, in addition to reading phonetically. We were attending a denominational church regularly but deep **inside of me,** a hidden yearning was starting to build. But for **what?**

During this time I started attending a prayer group meeting once weekly; still later, I'd been asked by one of the pastors to teach four year old children after both of mine were attending school all day. Then one spring I was invited to teach some of the teachers the "nuts and bolts" of how to teach summer school. Still hunger and thirst increased and I began crying frequently, for no known reason to me.

Finally I made an appointment with my Pastor, because I would cry for inexplicable reasons and unexpectedly, yet it **wasn't** depression. However I was disappointed with myself about habit patterns which certainly needed reversals and with various undesirable reactions to incidents in life. The Pastor led us to Romans 6 and 7 and read portions. It couldn't have described me more accurately. However, neither one of us read or delved into these chapters far enough to see verse 25 in chapter 7 and on into chapter 8, verses 1 to 3, the **answer!** His Name is **Jesus** and His Blessed Holy Spirit. Pastor did make a few suggestions. Then it seemed Bible classes might be the treasures to reveal where the answer from the Lord Jesus lay. Would this reveal the mystery?

CHAPTER 10

---

# What Glorious Expertise
# In Ordering Our Steps!

So at church my first class was on Bible heroes while next door at the same time there was an evangelism class. One day as I waited before ours started, I overheard the Pastor in the other class ask what words should be **avoided** when witnessing lest they would **offend** people. My ears and heart were in disbelief, for can you guess what they were saying? Try, Dearly Beloved! Do you give up? The **fact** is they listed "born again," the Blood, sins and repentance. They continued in profusion on and on, listing the **very solid foundation** of the **truth** needed for salvation, redemption and walking as you grow, abandoning **carnal knowledge** to know Jesus more intimately.

Now, I was not in the class and you might say, "So what?" I realize the Holy Spirit might ease into His approach through you and you would not accuse people, but those words are a part of **salvation** and must not be **buried** or **omitted** but stated in truth! Also, it wasn't my business but the dark **deception** of Satan stabbed my heart and poured thoughts passionately in my mind for days, causing me to examine far more closely salvation from **God's** viewpoint. Eventually, the investigation resulted in my truly knowing the evil one **was** behind it!

What would be **essential** for people to know, I questioned over a period of time, since God is the "same yesterday, today, and forever?" Heb. 13:8 That **He had** clearly **initiated** a progressive covenant for us

72

throughout the Bible was evident. More was revealed when He found a man in Genesis 12, who **believed** Him, therefore initiating the beginning of restoration of the **intended** plan for the **first** Adam. Do you realize that Abram believed God, by **not** listening to **any** other voices and yet he lived in an atmosphere where idols were worshipped and his father was an idolater? Josh. 24:2 Abraham reached such a point that "20He staggered not at the promise of God through unbelief; but was strong in faith, giving glory to God; 21and being fully persuaded that, what He had promised, He was able also to perform." Rom. 4 KJV Astonishingly, he did not **stagger** but **grew** in **faith** and believed God to **fullness** of persuasion.

I strongly believe, though not precisely stated in Scripture, that since he'd been in Satan's realm in Ur, Satan, because of his persistent despicable personality, would **not loose** him willingly without a struggle! That he would continue with his wicked, misleading attempts to keep him snared under his influence, for he sticks like epoxy to those he has ensnared! God did **command** that he **leave** his father behind, probably so He could change Abram's thinking more easily when removed from his life in Ur, where Satan dominated with so many temptations. There are some cities or areas where the Body of Christ has allowed him to run rampant even in the United States, but we are awakening and taking our God-given authority.

Another class John and I took together at night was unusually interesting and one entailing Biblical **principles, concepts** and **truths pictured creatively.** Admirably it was borrowed from another mainline church, lasting two **years** and meeting once weekly. The first year included the **entire** Old Testament, while the second included the **entire** New Testament. One outstanding feature was that the Hebrew language is practical, utilizing basic root words upon which the others build, oftentimes developing **pictorial** ones, making it appealing to remember. This in turn makes the parables of Jesus more vivid! Later when Blessing the homes and businesses, the Holy Spirit often exposed where the enemy's work had destroyed creativity, **frequently** unrealized by the people.

In our Better Covenant we are commanded to **renew** or **transform** our minds. Rom. 12:1-3 My first book *The Victor's Mind Can Be Yours* gives more details about this. Abram **did** have to drive off vultures right after God visited him. Gen. 15:11 Then He added **blood** sacrifice to the covenant, revealing to us that following spiritual and obedient words and actions, the enemy moves in with attacks quickly! I call God's Covenant **progressive,** because of the additions **God** initiates, gradually increasing our understanding and knowledge, building like living blocks what He had already completely finished in His Plan for us before the foundation of the world. Eph. 1

There are other covenants in the Bible which Almighty God had, such as the ones with Adam, Job and Noah. But each was very limited and those of us grafted into the Better Covenant know it is built on Abraham's covenant! Alleluia!

It is written in Psalm 37, AMP "23The steps of a [good] man are directed *and* established of the Lord, when He delights in his way [and He busies Himself with his every step]. 24Though he fall, he shall not be utterly cast down, for the Lord grasps his hand in support *and* upholds him." I'm certain Dear Reader, you can see this in the life of Abram, the care and love given to him by Father God, so you will see more and more His care for you as well. It is so amazing Abram became "fully persuaded that, what He had promised, He was able also to perform." Rom. 4:21 KJV Please remember Almighty God was able and willing with two older people involved as well!

God then changed Abram's name to Abra**ha**m, giving him a part of Jehov**ah**'s Name, meaning "a father of many nations" Gen. 17:5 and he became our Father of Faith on earth! Gal. 3:7 Thanks be to God that the Gentiles (non-Jews) were grafted into The Vine, our Lord and King Jesus! Next He promised and commanded, "10This *is* My covenant which you shall keep, between Me and you and your descendants after you: Every male child among you shall be circumcised; 11and you shall be circumcised in the flesh of your foreskins, and it shall be a sign of the covenant between Me and you." Gen. 17 In **every** male this is where the seed is stored physically obviously for procreation, but also establishing as **fact** that **blood** is to be a vital part of every covenant He initiates, a shadow of the Better Covenant to come, because "the life of the flesh *is* in the blood." Lev. 17:11

After this first command, this was to continue being done throughout the generations to all male babies on the **eighth** day after birth and doctors today have caught up with God, by discovering **less** blood is shed if done on **that exact** day! Almighty God without a doubt places immense value on every word in the Holy Bible! As He once told me, **"Every Word In the Bible is covered with My Blood."** What that tells me is to see and hear every single word, for each is significant and interwoven into an entire gigantic and eternal plan, ever revealing more truth!

Gloriously, as I said, it's a shadow of the **Better Covenant** where the Blood of Jesus is the Life of the Spiritual part of us, the Body of Christ! That is exactly why Jesus said, when He took the cup at the Last Supper with His disciples, "This cup *is* the new covenant in My Blood, which is shed for you." Luke 22:20 Much more regarding the **Better Covenant** between God and Jesus is revealed in Hebrews! We can be ignorant of it, completely disregard it or make comments about our improvised opinions, because of what we may think, but none of these comments or attitudes **alter** or **affect** the actual Blood Covenant!

Meditate about this, please! Every tribe and nation throughout the world has more or less some understanding of **blood** covenant, which is serious and **if** broken by man is unto **death** in many cultures. Now even though Satan lived with God, until pride and wickedness entered his thinking, swallowing his goodness, he was still totally ignorant concerning the blood. You see a fallen angel has no blood or heart, so the Blood of Jesus becomes an **inspired** and **supernatural** tool against him. He fears the power of It because It is **alive** and **speaks!** Don't ask me **how** the **Blood is** still alive and speaks. But **It is** and **does!** Because our Heavenly Father wants a family who truly loves **Him,** He planted in each person a **heart desire** for fellowship with Him and one another! Frequently though people fail to recognize what is truly lacking in their lives! But Satan is all hatred and will always come against God. The most awesome news is that God's Better **New Testament Covenant cannot** be broken by man, because it was cut between Almighty God and Jesus.

Contemplate how our enemy has tried to eradicate, pervert or discredit every plan and relationship with human beings and the One Living Great Creator. You can recognize every action of his, because each attempts "to steal, and to kill, and to destroy" John 10:10 purity and morality from people or God's Words and reputation. Today he has people in the cults literally drinking people's or animals' blood; he tries to corrupt the pure covenant relationship between two covenant friends, for example David and Jonathan in the Bible. 1 Samuel 18

Also, he has perverted relationships between God and His people, as well as between parents and children, between men with men as well as women with women, over and over **wherever** he can gain a foothold. He even tries to convince human beings through lies that they have been created **peculiarly** perverse and cannot be normal in their thinking and living, as Father God designed them! The enemy surely has succeeded repeatedly, all because of pride, hate and all possible wickedness.

Once in one of the homes that I was spiritually blessing by exposing the undercover antics of our enemy, the Holy Spirit used the name "Beelzebub" to purge an ugly and bountiful swarm of wild **flies** on a staircase! When the whole house was spiritually Blessed and we returned to the stairs, there were **dead** flies everywhere! Glory to God! Later when I rechecked the name in the Bible, remembering it was one of Satan's names, used derogatorily against our Precious Lord, I discovered he was a Philistine deity! Matt. 10:25 He is also called "the ruler of the demons" Mark 3:22 and *The New Strong's Expanded Exhaustive Concordance of the Bible Red-Letter Edition* adds he's called a "dung-god." No wonder flies usually frequent such dirty places on earth. Wasn't the Holy Spirit precious to do such **quick** work? The authority and power given to us by Jesus against our insidious enemy is far greater than all he concocts! Luke 10:19 AMP Do continue listening attentively to the Holy Spirit, for those who listen and follow the Holy Spirit become the sons of God! Rom. 8:14 It is such an **exciting** walk in the spirit.

Speaking of names of our enemy, Almighty God **gradually** revealed in 1988, only **four specific** and **prominent** names used by Satan worshippers, which were confirmed by three of his devotees and in the Satanic bible! His bible calls them Crown Princes. Studying them briefly as led by the Holy Spirit, I saw all four names are in our Bibles! As a result, **rebuking** their names, when it is obvious that their evil antics are operating through people or situations, will **often** manifest **instant** results! But ask the Holy Spirit to reveal every time what is to be done.

You have undoubtedly detected God is **very** serious about the names of people fitting their personalities! Do you recall Jesus renaming Peter? The same is true of the demons, for their names are descriptive of their wicked works. One name is **Belial,** whose name personifies lawlessness, wickedness and rebellion; he is called the Crown Prince of the North and ruler of the earth by his master. He is also involved with magic. In our Bibles "daughter, men, sons, children of Belial" are referred to as lawless ones. God says "For rebellion *is as* the sin of witchcraft." 1 Sam. 15:23 "Mount Zion on the sides of the north" is referred to as "the city of the great King," Psa. 48:1-3; Isa. 14:13 and is described as belonging to God, so it seems clear that rebellion would run rampant from the north in a broad sense but the Holy Spirit is the One to consult.

**Satan** is referred to as the Crown Prince of the South and the lord of the **fire.** We know he is wicked, 1 John 2:13 the accuser of the brethren, Rev. 12:10 a liar, a master of deception, John 8:44 and a blinder of the eyes of unbelievers. 2 Corinth. 4:3-4 He deserves hell, so he is lord there! On earth we clobber him when demons are obviously evident.

I suspect his name could be used against arson and against the demons perpetuating it, to stop it **at once** in arsonists, too. I have an amazing incident to tell! I was attending a Spirit-filled Methodist Church where a man **testified!** Once when his barn was burning, he came against Satan and the fire died down, but he would **stop** using his authority and the flames would blaze **anew.** He'd use his authority again and the same thing happened repeatedly. Satan is persistent! Do not fear or ignore him, just **terminate** his antics.

The third Crown Prince is **Lucifer** of the East and is spirit ruler of the air! Eph. 2:2 Isaiah 14 truly exposes him; he even imitates the True Light of the World, John 8:12 our most Precious Jesus. 2 Corinth. 11:14 He weakened nations, destroyed cities, "made the world as a wilderness" Isa. 14:17 and more evil besides. He is truly **personified** pride, greed and destruction to me! You may be thinking of some false religions from the East or objects bought as souvenirs, which can be an invitation to the enemy. It seems obvious when to use authority strongly against him, but we are **not** to dwell on the enemy, but to invite the Holy Spirit to reveal when and how to pray, declare and decree, using this name.

The last one is **Leviathan,** the Crown Prince of the West and ruler of the sea. His name in Hebrew comes from two words meaning "joined" and "dragon." He's a troublemaker, brings despair, is haughty, merciless and he twists situations. I have not a clear usage of him, so keep on asking the Holy Spirit. It is important to know that these four names are worshipped by those believers in Satan as revealed in the Satanic bible. They help keep perpetuating addictions of many kinds as well as suicides. So again let's stay alert and share with others when led by the Holy Spirit. Let's tromp on them using our God-given authority from Jesus!

# CHAPTER 11

# Christ Is There All the Time!

Are you thinking of ways God has already been leading **you?** Sometimes the steps are small and so carefully orchestrated by God, you see them in hindsight perfectly! How God weaves everything together for multitudes of His children at the same time, resulting in His **very** best for each involved in His **big** plan, realizing this almost boosts me like a kite. I'm continuing to show more ways He ordered my steps, so you can have even **greater** understanding and awe-inspiring appreciation in your own walk in the spirit and love! A Scripture which truly opened my eyes early in my walk and still continues to help me, coupled with Psalm 37:23-24 mentioned in the last chapter, is Proverbs 16:9, AMP "A man's mind plans his way, but the Lord directs his steps *and* makes them sure." **Only His** ideas succeed in my life so I request His veto whenever I'm off track!

When I was still attending the church mentioned, I was driving from town to our home and was at a stop light, when I glanced right at a used car lot. At this time in our lives we were still buying used cars, because early in our marriage I quickly, literally **hated** "time payments" of any kind. I had tried **once** with a set of Encyclopedia Britannicas and was fed up in several months; no fun at all. I spotted a yellow station wagon in the lot and said aloud, "There's our car." When I told John about it, we agreed God would provide an honest salesman before we knew the power of agreement established by God, and with great ease it became our car. God's idea planted in me!

One day after attending this particular church for about thirteen years, I discovered a fairly new Christian book store, planted in an attractive older home in the city! I wandered into one room **not** realizing **what** I needed, but the manager Walt, newly baptized in the Holy Spirit, came to me and said, "May I help you find something?" Words poured out from a **hungry** and **thirsty heart, "Jesus** is **not real** enough to me!" This surprised me, for **consciously** I did **not** know what was amiss. He handed me John Sherrill's book *They Speak with Other Tongues!* He continued, "If you have questions after you read it, do come see me!" It is an **extremely** helpful, clearly written book with Scriptures proving the truths and helped to take blinders off my mind, ears and eyes, resulting in true understanding!

Believe me I read it as rapidly as I could, looking up **every single** Scripture, which was listed very neatly in about the center of the author's adventure in his investigation of this often neglected, but never rescinded **command** by Christ! I chewed and swallowed the Word voraciously. After dropping the children off at school one morning, a few **days** later, I drove back to see Walt **before** his store opened. By this time, he had moved to a larger store with a good-sized prayer room; I pounded on the door and screeched loudly, because I knew he prayed inside before the store opened. This was **not** my nature, in fact, he called me mousey up to this point. I quickly drove around several blocks, which seemed to **devour** an **eternity,** hurriedly attacked the door again and he came from across the street. I was very rude, yelling, "Where have you been?" for hunger and thirst had swallowed me. He graciously taught me for an hour and a half what **God knew** I needed and he kept on, even though the store had opened. I had walked right over the truth which I was pursuing. He told me **later** God said, **"Do not lay hands on her for she is Mine!"** Alleluia!

That night, when my husband came home, he could see the reality, anointing and the glory of Jesus in my eyes and face. I didn't even think to (nor could I) hold back anything. So I explained excitedly what had happened, told the children what I was seeking and that night after they were put to bed and the evening chores done very quickly, I poured over the Scriptures again. Rereading each **Scripture** I told Father God, **"If the Baptism of the Holy Spirit will make me a better Christian**, please **fill** me!"** Immediately a **volcanic** eruption of living water gushed forth from inside for almost two hours, as more and more unknown words came pouring forth but **no** English! John 7:38-39 AMP Isaiah 12:3-4, "3Therefore with joy you will draw water from the wells of salvation. 4And in that day you will say: 'Praise the Lord, call upon His name; Declare His deeds among the peoples, Make mention that His Name is exalted,' " truly kept bubbling in my heart.

The **peace** of God overwhelmed and filled me, as a **living** well overflowing and "joy unspeakable and full of glory" 1 Pet. 1:8 KJV continually poured forth. I even woke up my son **upstairs,** for he called out "Mom, did you get **it?"** meaning the Baptism of the Holy Spirit. I surely did! Did you note **Isaiah** was not led to say, "We were to be **real quiet** and not share about God and "His deeds among the peoples?" Where do you think that idea initiated? When you are baptized in the Holy Spirit, you open your spirit and your soul to a greater anointing in power and authority, enabling you to yield more to the Holy Spirit's guidance 1 John 2:20, 27 and you really can't keep things like effervescent joy hidden! This will do wonders in restoring your relationship with Daddy God. This so beautifully confirmed for me what Almighty God had told Walt.

For days and days sleep was of no interest, so mercifully God arranged for John through his work schedule to be out of town for **six weeks.** Alleluia! That had never happened before nor since and it was almost long enough. Glory! This way I could get more saturation of the precious Scriptures day and night and my husband was not disturbed! Much later I discovered the song of the passage above! Truth, truth, truth!

Proverbs 19:21, "Many plans are in a man's mind, but it is the Lord's purpose for him that will stand." AMP I say even more so for the hungry and thirsty, needy ones! I was like Joseph, for I told everyone, so deeply desirous for others to share His sparkling joy, and to partake of greater freedom in Christ. "Freely (without pay) you have received, freely (without charge) give." Matt. 10:8 AMP **"Praise the Lord"** very frequently poured out from my spirit for weeks. It now flowed out naturally; I would answer the phone and out came "Praise the Lord." Now I understood why it appears so often in the Psalms. We have heaps and heaps for which to be very thankful and will never be able to thank Him sufficiently. "A happy heart is good medicine *and* a cheerful mind works healing, but a broken spirit dries up the bones." Prov 17:22 AMP

Another unique way Almighty God ordered my steps was through inviting me to teach classes In the second church again I was asked to teach children's Sunday school for five and six year olds. After some years, once more I was asked to teach **adult** women's classes on pointers regarding how to teach. Many times I had said to my friend Ethel, that I'd like to sing in the choir and she tired of my saying it so often (I hadn't realized how often) and asked "What are you waiting for — an engraved invitation?" That **very** evening the choir director called and asked if I'd like to sing in the choir. I wasted no time in joining! I suspect Ethel was delighted and relieved!

In the process of Ethel discipling (mentoring) me, she was asked by our Pastor to visit a Swiss lady who attended the church we were in; I had started driving her to various places at God's direction, though I was unaware of it, assisting God's widow indeed, for Ethel's husband had graduated to Heaven. This fulfilled the verse in James 1:27, Wuest

"Religion which is pure and undefiled in the sight of God, even the Father, is this: to look after orphans and widows in their affliction with a view to ascertaining their needs and supplying them, and to be keeping one's self unspotted from the world." For many years after driving Ethel places, when she moved and also graduated to Heaven, I acquired two other widows whom I just took on drives weekly around the countryside. Father God revealed **very** recently that this was one reason why He brought in **all** the funds to pay for the cost of my first book without my asking. He cares **deeply** about **orphans** and **widows!**

Sometime later I was asked to teach on the Holy Spirit by a friend Barbara in her home, followed by teaching on the Holy Spirit in another friend's home, Katrin, from a year long syllabus of John Decker's. With John's course, I was allowed to add teaching about our Better Covenant in the New Testament and the Blood. I recall one day in the middle of the teaching about the Blood, I started repeating, **very** strongly, "the Blood of Jesus" several times! I was standing facing the hallway leading to one bedroom. Later, I was told that every time I repeated the phrase, Katrin's husband Welles felt a surge of power and healing. I didn't know this until afterwards, for he was in bed not feeling well at the time. If we are willing to yield and turn God loose, He can accomplish so much more and how the **excitement escalates!**

Yet in another home and time, I was teaching the same course and the gracious lady of the home had a pet bird, who loved to sing when I was teaching. Marilyn and I were there together and she was binding every foul demon she could, as I taught, but that **bird** kept singing! I loved it; but the lady removed it from the room, so the rest of the women around the table would not be distracted. Lo and behold when I listened to the tape, I had been teaching on the wonderful **authority** of the **believer** given to us by our Lord Jesus. We had a hearty laugh, though quite obviously we needed to understand much more. Today I'm still learning but I've come down the pathway quite a ways, thanks to Abba Father, Jesus my Lord and the Teacher of the Body of Christ, the Holy Spirit.

# CHAPTER 12

## My World Turns
## Right Side UP

Everything changed drastically from that evening on, after I received the Baptism in the Holy Spirit, I mean **radically!** People would stop by unexpectedly, many prayers were quickly answered through the prayer chain I was heading, and schedules were upset, whirling around like a tornado! **Everything** that happened became exciting, **nothing** was annoying in any way, in fact, flexibility in all my plans flew like a shooting Roman candle! Everything was thrilling yet peaceful. Others in the prayer group at church were filled with the Holy Spirit to overflowing at about the same time, 2 Corinth. 5:17 AMP so nothing was the same there either. Luke 3:16 As a most **enormous** hunger for the Word of God literally consumed us, we shared books being devoured like a dog gobbles his food — fast and furiously. When the prayer group met we would literally dump **arm loads** of books on the table "up for grabs and trade" even before we prayed!

After some weeks I became a thorn in the Pastor's life, whose wife and him I deeply loved, because of several messages inspired by the Holy Spirit in **small** gatherings. One did pertain to the importance of the Blood of Jesus! The crux of the matter resulted in an anointed message I was ordered by the Lord to give, lasting **one minute,** at the end of a regular service! (When I received the Baptism in the Holy Spirit, I had told his wife and him I would stay **quiet.**) After falling on my knees, praying in a solitary place, I almost flew to an Assembly of God church where I knew several ladies would pray with me. I had agreed I'd be quiet, a **big** mistake for I was unaware of God's plan.

You may be inquiring what I said. It was "God is moving mightily by His Spirit throughout the earth!" Failing to ask permission to speak, I spoke a few words in tongues and sat down, but not interrupting and still within the one minute. The service had started out powerfully with four lively trumpets and the hymn, *God of Our Fathers, Whose Almighty Hand.* About a week later I went to get a copy of the sermon because I thought it was tied in with God's message. It was *Are You Willing To Be Made A Fool For Christ?*

Though not for long, I was constrained by the Holy Spirit to stay at the church, and after several weeks, when Pastor was ready, we discussed the event at our home. Though we had attended for thirteen years I left as much for Pastor's sake as mine. Prior to meeting with the Pastor however, a local doctor called and said he and his uncle, visiting him from another state, had been praying for me and thought my hubby and I should come and visit them. Though John declined, I did go; the men were gracious but advised I should have met with the Pastor and asked him prior to the actual event or tell him the message before I delivered it.

For Pastor's sake I most likely should have; but I have observed after many years since then, I have at times been led by Father God to be a **catalyst** to stimulate scrutinizing the Scriptures with an open mind and perhaps assist in transforming minds of others, as we are commanded. Rom. 12:1-2 AMP In meditating on some of the words spoken by Jesus to people, He was a catalyst, too. It is difficult to withstand the ideas of others sometimes, but when you're certain it's God, **obey!** He often withholds the reason and the outcome until the obedience is **fulfilled.** This **builds** trust in Him!

87

Also, I was told a Sunday school teacher that very morning told his class that **Almighty God** had spoken in church today, resulting in his teaching some of the Scriptures **not** usually taught by this particular denomination! I don't know who the teacher was, but the mother of a child in his class called to tell me her child was very excited.

How precious of our Heavenly Father, Almighty God, when one has been asked to do perhaps a more difficult task than some, to allow us after the fact to know at least one positive blessing resulted! I refer to this as Almighty God balancing His scales with "righteousness and justice" for us, Gen. 18:19 when **obedience** has required **more courage** and **boldness.** As we mature in Him it seems His commands gradually become more intense. It's important to be led by the Holy Spirit, when leaving a church, and to depart with no **hostility** or **hurts,** so you can walk in love and the spirit and be a blessing wherever you go, so no fragmented relationships are left behind. Then you can join a new congregation with **closed** lips and a clean slate! We are to love each person and even more deeply with *agapé* love, especially our brothers and sisters in Christ. 1 John 4:7-8, 21

Shortly after the Holy Spirit Baptism, I began playing taped messages, for many women once weekly, of well-known Spirit-filled apostles and teachers such as Dennis Bennett, because John and I were aware of his night classes of teaching regarding the Holy Spirit! We had attended them, when they were held regularly at St. Luke's Episcopalian Church that Dennis reopened in Seattle. A number of hungry men and women came and we each benefited greatly, for we were partaking like little children of a **new** variety of **fresh** bread from Heaven (Jesus), which was very accurate scripturally. Alleluia!

John went one night to a weekly meeting of Father Bennett's to receive the Baptism of the Holy Spirit about seven months later than I, after which he said he sensed an **inner** "peace of God, which surpasses all understanding." Phil. 4:7 In addition, I signed up for a series of corre-spondence classes from Moody Bible Institute. The first one was composed of memorization of **seventy-eight** Scriptures; **every single one** has been **foundational** in my life since then. Heb. 4:12 Obviously the choice was of God!

Life was increasingly busy but most energetic, spiritually very grat-ifying and interspersed with powerful miracles, thanks be to Father God! Almighty God initiated a number of trips to innumerable **enrich-ing** and **life changing** spiritual meetings and Christian ministries, two located overseas — one in Scotland (mentioned earlier) and the other in Latvia and Moscow with Rick Renner Ministries. In the USA the trips were from California to Colorado to Georgia to Florida to Texas to Missouri and Seattle. Locally He led me to attend various churches, revealing a broad spectrum of diversified assignments within the Body of Christ. I surely can be referred to as a person deeply in love with our Lord Jesus, a Christian or a "baptimethopresbycostalinternondal."

I've been blessed by being allowed to do His calling, by His proph-esying, teaching, praying and ministering to individuals through me. In Proverbs 31:26 early in my walk, it was revealed through the Holy Spirit to mine, but also through a prophet publicly, that I desperately needed to apply this verse of the virtuous woman, "She opens her mouth with skillful and godly Wisdom, and in her tongue is the law of kindness — giving counsel and instruction." AMP Years later it had been interwoven enough I could teach it to twelve women in church, for there is much in this Scripture to be taken literally but spiritually, too.

I reremember as well after some growth in the Lord, when I first was touched in my heart by 1 Samuel 3:19, "So Samuel grew, and the Lord was with him and let none of his words fall to the ground." My prayer request became that **none** of my words, especially given to others, would fall to the ground because they were initiated by God.

This was after I had to learn to be **extremely** careful about every word I spoke, in that they would be His words for them and not of me. I still am being very careful of my words. But first I had to learn "Therefore, my beloved brethren, let every man be swift to hear, slow to speak, slow to wrath." James 1:19 Later I learned that **every one** of our **words** are **containers** and **never** die. I had heard years before that scientists someway discovered the words of Dwight Moody in his pulpit! Truth!

In some churches I was inspired and permitted to lead songs for the congregation to sing, to give words publicly and privately for exhortation, or I was given songs from the Holy Spirit with words like a bubbling brook, often bubbles, bubbles, bubbles bursting forth, resulting in joy permeating many hearers. To my delight I **was** hearing and giving the words of the Holy Spirit, for one day I discovered in the notes on Psalm 45:1 that the Hebrew for "overflowing" ("inditing" in KJV) means "boil or bubble up." The actual verse is "My heart is overflowing with a good theme; I recite my composition concerning the King; my tongue *is* the pen of a ready writer."

In **many gatherings** sometime later, holy laughter initiated by the Blessed Holy Spirit erupted spontaneously, being freely spilled out uncontrollably as part of freeing God's people. In the early 1990's, when I was reading 1 Corinthians 14:40, "Let all things be done decently and in order," God told me **"Mary, My order is not parallel to nor like man's (order) necessarily."** Some years later He enlightened me even more to inquire of Him what **is** of **Him,** when things are happening in the congregation and pay careful attention to the checks inside my spirit from the Holy Spirit, so that I don't say, "Well, that is not of God," when it really is.

Several years prior to this I had seen a vision, as Psalm 139 was being read aloud by Rita Bennett in a gentle meeting, where we were invited to listen attentively to the Holy Spirit as she read it and after she finished! Jesus appeared to me in a vision — I saw His feet in sandals, as He was behind me, in a local park. There He offered to push me, sitting in one of the swings, as long as I **liked.** Jesus my Lord and elder Brother was near me; I was so overwhelmed with appreciation, I shortened the time much faster than I really desired. He said, **"Let us walk to a picnic table,"** which was near-by.

He stood behind me, as I sat down where I spotted a large wad of old gray clay on the table, like I had used in grade school. As I put my hands on it, He placed His muscular, larger hands over mine, starting to shape the clay and asking me, **"May I do with you what I want to do?"** I knew, because of Jeremiah 18, which though applied to the "house of Israel," v6 He was relating and applying it to my life v4 asking if He could have carte blanche with my life! So I said, "Yes!" He quickly formed a tall slender vase. As He worked I did notice there were some dried pieces in the clay — two were implanted flat and the third was embedded perpendicularly to the foot of the vase. Then He was gone!

Eight days later, on a Saturday, I was led to call to see if I could attend a one day seminar in Seattle at a place called Burden Bearers; I did not know why. **Varying** from the normal procedure, the counselor **answered** the phone when I called, as directed by the Holy Spirit, and she said I could attend even if I might arrive late. On the way, as I drove there, the Holy Spirit told me to respond when the counselor asked for people to share. Soon after my arrival the counselor said there **were** two men and two women who were to share, as God had told them.

We four did reveal what the Holy Spirit led us to tell, after being screened by the leadership first, a great safeguard. We volunteered what we heard from the Holy Spirit; my very recent experience **was** my topic. Immediate responses were made regarding the meaning of the dry pieces of clay. The really embedded piece of clay represented condemnation and guilt over my parents' divorce, for instance. After additional ministry to me, they asked what I was seeing! My vase was skinny as well as taller, painted very quickly, whereupon it was put into a kiln. One woman immediately spoke out boldly, "And not one strand of hair nor her eyelashes will be singed." This statement probably was based on Daniel 3:25-27. "[27]And the satraps, administrators, governors, and the king's counselors gathered together, and they saw these men on whose bodies the fire had no power; the hair of their head was not singed nor were their garments affected, and the smell of fire was not on them."

Also Daddy God is revealing to us **more** about His mighty protection in Isaiah 43. "[1]He who formed you, O Israel: 'Fear not, for I have redeemed you; I have called *you* by your name; you *are* Mine. [2]When you pass through the waters, I *will be* with you; and through the rivers, they shall not overflow you. When you walk through the fire, you shall not be burned, nor shall the flame scorch you. [3]For I *am* the Lord your God, The Holy One of Israel, your Savior; [7]Everyone who is called by My name, Whom I have created for My glory; I have formed him, yes, I have made him.' "

Though God is speaking here to Israel, we are to appropriate the words because Jesus has redeemed those who accept Him as Lord and Savior! Now there are no more unexplainable tears! Now tears come often and easily in gratitude and **countless** thankfulness for all Father God has done, including giving me a perfect Father, Who knows me better than anyone else ever can and corrects me perfectly! [Heb. 12:9-11] There are tears in intercession as well occasionally which I welcome.

# CHAPTER 13

# Mr. Serendipity

Some months after my Baptism in the Holy Spirit, **Ethel** came to our home and taught an awe-inspiring teaching on *The Name of Jesus*, because we needed to **know** Him better and the **tremendous power** in the privilege of the usage of His precious Name. Very few people I knew then had any knowledge or understanding of what Jesus had accomplished after His sacrifice on the Cross, of His perfect obedience, saying **only** what Father God said and doing **only** what Father God did, John 12:49-50 resulting in His crucifixion as part of **God's plan!**

Because of our Lord's perfect obedience, Beloved, so much happened. His exceedingly precious Blood was shed so many places prior to the Cross and on the Cross; after He died He was put in a heavily sealed tomb; He departed and went to hell; He took the captives with Him who had been protected in Paradise until His resurrection; He defeated **all** the powers of hell and took them captive, making a public display in the heavenlies in **triumphing** over them! Col. 2:15 There are **no** adequate words to describe all our coming King did for every person ever born on earth!

Being able to **know** I truly was **hearing** the Holy Spirit after I started training my spirit to listen ceaselessly in expectancy, almost every single breath I took became an exhilaratingly joyous experience including today. About thirteen years after I received the Baptism in the Holy Spirit, I became involved with answering phones locally for The

700 Club and developed in hearing Him even **more** acutely, due to a specific anointing from God, because many times the people themselves didn't know what God, Jesus and the Holy Spirit needed to accomplish **first** through or for them. Countless times the person and I were both surprised. It was my grateful pleasure to learn even more through taking a class from John Decker called Christ's Institute for Ambassadors. But hang on, I've fast forwarded a few years, so I'll rewind back about thirteen.

Immediately after the dynamic change, from the gathering of cars around our cul-de-sac at times, even the neighborhood children knew things were **popping.** So they would come to my door, telling me about problems that needed prayer, or other heart concerns, sometimes even with injured birds, so all of us would pray! My rocking chair frequently became the "miracle chair" for those of any age — male or female — needing faith prayers, blessings, or ministry of some kind. It was most delicious and very constant, but yet the housework got done! "O taste and see that the Lord [our God] is good! Blessed — happy, fortunate, [to be envied] — is the man who trusts *and* takes refuge in Him." Psa. 34:8 AMP

One early evening on the Fourth of July a whirling fire-wheel nailed in a post spun off and went right under our neighbor's car! My spirit exploded rapidly with no thought about any effect on others and I sounded out very loudly, "In the Name of Jesus the car is protected, in the Name of Jesus" and again "in the Name of Jesus!" It was indeed safe! Glory to God.

Another late afternoon about eight young girls were in our living room so long that two of their Moms came over to investigate and sample what was underway. While the two boys ran around our house playing, the girls were **praying** regarding a Satanic church, for an ornery boy they knew and other things on their hearts. With the Baptism of the Holy Spirit comes an **acute** awareness of the authority our Lord Jesus turned over to us, when He returned to Heaven and released precious compassion, a gift from Jesus for others, hidden in us at first!

Later we discovered one husband next door was in his prayer closet all the time that particular night while we had been in prayer and praise! **Suddenly** as we prayed each girl commenced crying, so the only thing I knew to do was pray for the Baptism of the Holy Spirit! As a result I asked each Mom to minister to several girls! They **all** received and started being power temples for the Lord from then on! 1 Corinth. 6:19

That year on the Sunday just before Thanksgiving, one of the daughters next door took off with her boy friend, we knew not where, so we three mothers — neighbors on each side — prayed and the Lord God revealed that surely she would be thinking about her family gathering together because of Thanksgiving and would call. Right after the prayer, the mothers started talking about how it might happen but yet **how** could it?! I was rude saying, how could He work with doubt poisoning the air and so quickly? Besides, God does takes care of the **how** any way **He** desires if we **stay out** of His way and we don't need to try figuring it out! Prov. 3:5 AMP God's faithfulness considered how **green** we were in understanding in our minds, yet our **hearts** were filled with faith **when** we prayed! I was so delighted because a double-minded person gets nothing from the Lord. James 1:6-8 On Thanksgiving Day the first thing the call came from California and the father took off to bring back the adventuresome couple! Glory!

Our Father yearns to protect us and give only His best for each of us and our families! So "Let us therefore come boldly to the throne of grace, that we may obtain mercy and find grace to help in time of need." Heb. 4:16 So we will be asking and **expecting** an **answer** always! *"Now the just shall live by faith; but if anyone draws back, My soul has no pleasure in him."* Heb. 10:38 For the veil has been torn (top to bottom),

Matt. 27:51 at His sacrifice on the Cross from the top (Heaven) to bottom (earth) and His Blood has restored and prepared the way for us to "come boldly to the throne of grace" Heb. 4:16 and God.

Be led by the Holy Spirit because He knows best what should be asked for or how and when to utilize any verse in Scripture. He brings knowledge deep from within each spirit, though understanding may or may not be revealed, and sometimes the answer might even **surprise you.** As was mentioned, that's one of the extraordinary qualities, uniqueness and delights of our precious Lord!

Remember you are in perfect **union** with the Father, Son and Holy Spirit so you really are **His power temple,** in fact your body belongs to God! 1 Corinth. 6:19-20 But do we believe it? If we knew exactly how everything would be done, He would not be Almighty God, would He? I lovingly call Him **"Mr. Serendipity!"**

Besides He **delights** in amazing us through others. For many years John and I would put our feet down during the night after heavy rains on our concrete floor in the basement bedroom, intermittently we'd even splash in water, until we gained **victory** the majority of the time. (Upstairs it took years to gain success over abundant water hammering through our windows as well.) One day a week I was gone most of the day at church and on one very **special** day, when I came home there stood my son John and his wife, Tricia, smiling very broadly at me, inviting me to go downstairs. Can you guess what was there? They had purchased and installed a plush carpet on our cold, cold floor! There they waited with a camera! What a treat and pleasure it has been for years now!

More than once someone would surprise me by planting flowers. One woman came, brought her children and **secretly** planted beautiful plants on our front entry landing outdoors! What a present! My daughter Suzanna and her husband, Saúl, have done the same thing innumerable times with a variety of colors and kinds, some planted in rows like soldiers. They have blessed us as well with Christmas trees and even our adopted sweet princess, red ribbon and all — our Dalmatian, Shasta!

After some time my Mother had moved to our area about twenty miles north of us to a pretty mobile home park, nestled on a quiet knoll almost in the country, overlooking a gorgeous valley. One evening in the fall, I was driving to see her for a visit, when on the scenic back road there stood a large horse munching grass along the roadside, so I knew to try to be of assistance in protecting it. I drove to one near-by home, nestled far back from the road and asked if they knew whose horse it was. After my identifying it, he said "He's mine and is a very expensive one." So he went to get a rope and I drove him back to his treasure. You can be so certain, when you're led by the Holy Spirit that you are safe and ordinary things become **extraordinary!**

I recall once when Father God was surprising me by suggesting something very expensive, which didn't seem practical. He spoke very firmly, **"Mary, I'm extravagant!"** I chewed on that for a time, remembering how true it seemed, as I meditated on diverse episodes in the Bible. Truth! Another time I needed to spend some time away from everything and away from my home, alone in prayer and fellowship with God somewhere! Proclaiming boldly to my friends if I could spend only **twenty** dollars a night for **four** nights, I surely would go! Several people laughed at me, but I had some serious situations to share with God alone.

Yes! Yes! Yes! I was allowed to stay in a room by myself in a huge lodge called Rainbow, representing God's Covenant to me, in a wooded area about twenty-five miles away. I was alone in the sleeping quarters upstairs with two beds, one a loft-type, no phone (before cell phones) with just an eyelet lock on the door, (ha) while below my room with a balcony was the meeting place for large groups with a huge fireplace, as it was a **retreat** center. Free tea and coffee were made available to me in their huge kitchen, as they had a faucet producing instantaneous boiling water.

On Friday night a group moved in, but I had three days and nights **totally** alone with Father God. He can be extremely extravagant in varied ways. Truly I believe He honors our desire to be with Him, because of His eternal love for us. In Matthew 9:29 Jesus clearly states, "According to your faith let it be to you." Alleluia! It is truly one of my favorite verses, for it's pregnant with a broad range of possibilities galore.

Dearly Beloved Reader can you guess what was on the wall? An unusual picture with a swatch of colored yarns, framed attractively with **one** word on it. ??? **Serendipity!** There were many walking places in unoccupied land and a fish pond in the back yard. It was truly amazing in complete privacy and openness. During my stay I discovered the place was run by a Baptist minister, who offered to pray with me, if I wanted. Since then the gorgeous countryside is now built up with many large estate homes. But Daddy God had granted my heart and faith request in such an outstanding way!

Do you think we might miss amazing opportunities that God wants us to experience, because of His precious love for us and perhaps our failure to **apply faith** and **ask** Him at times? Let's be alert and ever listening! Very shortly after I was Holy Spirit Baptized, a visiting prophet, Dick Mills, gave me three verses from the Lord on asking — John 15:7, 1 John 3:21-22 and 1 John 5:14-15! Each had to do with asking and receiving **if** I was obedient and abiding in Him! It took a time of maturing, asking the Holy Spirit to direct **even** my questions before I fully appreciated those luxurious verses. They are overwhelmingly awesome in my heart today and forever! Beloved Friend, they are for you as well.

Wherever we are, whatever we're doing, be listening vigilantly for though Satan is **not ever** omnipresent, his cohorts are always on the lookout and hear more than we desire for sure. However, we have the **most powerful** tools against them — the Word, the Name of Jesus, His Blood and tongues — each of which do him harm as we **submit** ourselves to God, James 4:7 which he dreads. You can volunteer to read the Word to him, especially about his final demise, which slams his pride.

Also, when you are out and about in the market place, shopping or running errands, please do keep in mind to be alert by looking around and listening to the Holy Spirit, while speaking powerful words of victory and protection **ordered** by **God.** Sometimes when you are returning home, you may want to ask Abba Father if you need to come against the evil spirits, possibly encountered in your traveling for that is your responsibility. We always need to **focus** on God but keep our spiritual eyes open and our faith glasses on, guarding our hearts. Heb. 3:12-14; Phil. 4:6-7; 1 Pet. 3:15

This advice can surely be reinforced with a very recent experience qualifying as one of "the cares of this world." Mark 4:19 John and I were having a quiet time at home, after he had done many errands! I had made a rock-hard statement **aloud** that I was going to get to bed before midnight! Almost instantly thereafter our female Dalmatian dog went on a frantic and frenzied safari from room to room (at least six), making a scratching cluttered pile of each rug she could nest, including her own beds, acting as if she were going to give birth to puppies. She made **no** sounds but acted as if she were on an **unstoppable** assignment from another power! While on this **misadventure** her hair formed a **multitude** of tiny mountains all over her back and the sides of her body.

Abruptly I caught on that this was an abnormal attack from Satan's realm, so John and I started to fix his scheme! The Holy Spirit gave me the word **"Shalom, and come against anxiety,"** which I gladly said over and over again. It started calming her right away and we used the **Blood** against the attack and specifically against the bumps on her body. Then I stopped looking at her, believing our **agreement** prayer Matt. 18:18-20 was **in action!** After more "shaloms" and pattings were administered we started for bed. It was now almost 2:30 a.m., but I asked Father God, "What was behind this?" He replied, **"John brought home several devils, who thought they could perform some antics."** We quickly took care of them in faith with Scripture and the Blood.

A few hours later after sleeping well, all the pseudo signs were **completely** gone. In addition, a **very** precious surprise came as we read our normal daily Scripture for this victorious day, Proverbs 12:10, "A righteous *man* regards the life of his animal." Alleluia for our wondrous authority and "that we might be made the righteousness of God in Him." 2 Corinth. 5:21 KJV This could have resulted in the enemy stealing our sleep, our peace and money as well for the veterinarian. See John 10:10 and Matthew 13:18, Mark 4:13 and Luke 8:5.

Many times we don't enjoy **tongues** enough either, for I can testify that is a mighty **life line,** as well as a **perfect** prayer! Miracles themselves enter the picture, visions, dreams, words of wisdom and words of knowledge! Let's enjoy them more and more! You talk about exciting and fast results, as well as time saved on innumerable occasions. Do we really realize **everything God commands** us to do is **always beneficial** to us in far more ways than we will ever know and **often** prevents many problems as well?

# CHAPTER 14

## Miracles and Adventures Abound

To me it is a miracle for reborn human beings, God's creation, to be able to pray Holy Spirit initiated prayers accompanied by faith, His Gift, and receive answers that almost lift me off the ground in flight. Here are some unusual answers that you can have in abundance as well, for He has promised life **more** abundantly. John 10:10 Beloved, we do need to remember almost all of God's promises are contingent upon our obedience, which is just!

When I was helping the office staff in the church I was attending in the late 1980's, in the office where I worked I discovered a reference Bible which was very useful, being marked with color coding for Salvation, The Holy Spirit, Temporal Blessings and Prophetic Subjects. It was called a *New Marked Reference Bible*, but was out of print, the last date being 1983. I did know about a bookstore in Seattle which sells secondhand books, so I notified them and Marilyn, who assists me in countless ways, to keep scanning the shelves, whenever she was near books.

One day in 1991, about two years later, she was in a local Christian bookstore and there on the shelf **was** this **reference Bible.** When she asked the owner about it, it was **not even listed** in their records. In fact, the owner was amazed not ever having even **seen** it before! Thanks be to Almighty God and His caring, love and persistence, an angel had to have placed it there, because Daddy God delights to bless us often by giving treasures no one else could. If we're appreciative and keep in faith consistently, I believe He is **honored,** for I'm totally aware I **cannot** do these things by myself and prayers originated by the Holy Spirit are always answered in delightful ways. Besides a part of using our faith is stated **clearly** in Hebrews 11: 6, "*that* He is a rewarder of those who diligently seek Him." Let's not cancel out what **God** has said by our **false** humility! Why should our enemy steal God's rewards for his evil when we have the authority against him? Also, the more we gather the more we can give by being the Blessing we are called to be! Gen. 12 **In addition** some of my concocted prayers which have been answered from time to time were **not** desirable, so I've asked the Holy Spirit to please **veto all** my "flesh" prayers and correct me.

Another time, Marilyn and I were shopping in a different Christian bookstore, when one of my car doors was left unlocked. I had **just completed** highlighting all the verses pertaining to **"in Christ, in Him, with Him"** in a Bible **given** to me by Christ for the Nations, which was on the back seat of my car. When we returned after a brief shopping time, I saw **my** Bible was gone but Marilyn's was still there. After checking the store to be certain I'd not taken it with me, I demanded Satan return it or he owed me seven times what he'd stolen. Prov. 6:30-31 Now whenever I thought about it in the following weeks, I did declare **loudly** its return; yet about three months went by.

One morning **very** unexpectedly the phone rang, and a Christian woman I did not know said she had my Bible! She worked for a dentist about fifteen miles away and told me it had been found weeks before on the hood of a van, and had been brought into the office where it sat on a table all those missing weeks, thus being protected. Alleluia! She was given permission to call me about the Bible, finally; perhaps it was assumed I'd left it in the area. It also had so many inserts and markings written in it, it might have been intimidating to anyone opening it, unless he knew Jesus.

As I recall, Marilyn and I were able to conclude it must have been found the day it had been taken. In fact we both departed almost racing to pick it up after the call. It completely astonishes me how Father God and His angels do things for His believing children, and how very much He protects what **we** value, especially if we are grateful and free from greed and graspiness. The Word does work mightily, if we apply pressure, but as we can see with our children and friends gratitude is always appreciated. However, I focused on the Bible and should have gone **deeper** with Almighty God and inquired **why** only my Bible was stolen.

Very recently I was shown by the Holy Spirit through Billye Brim quoting John Lake, Kenneth Hagin, Sr. and Alexander MacLaren that the Body of Christ should **know** what vital accomplishments Jesus achieved by being persecuted on the Cross! What? His **total** victory in hell over the principalities, the powers, the rulers of darkness today and the wicked spirits in heavenly places, Eph. 6:12 then next, making a public display of conquering **all** of them. Col. 2:15 But we need revelation pertaining to what the **resurrection treasures** are, such as **knowing who** we are **in Christ,** and that we are seated **now** in Heavenly places positionally **with Christ** Eph. 2:6 **far above all** of them. Eph. 1:21

Also, **daily** it is an imperative necessity that we **apply** the **authority** and **power** given to us from our Head of the Body, Jesus our Lord and the Written Word and that we guard our words, so that many more disasters and tragedies can be avoided and prevented! These pointers do affect our future walk with Christ! In addition we are not fully utilizing the fullness of what Jesus accomplished by being crucified and defeating the evil spirits **for us** and we're failing in respecting Christ wholly! For example, sometimes God will entrust a vision to an active intercessor of a potential catastrophe, which can be prevented or changed if that person taps into the plan of Almighty God, proceeding as He directs. Also, **we** have the responsibility to **proclaim, declare** and **decree** before our High Priest far more than is realized, when initiated by the Holy Spirit! God and Jesus are depending on and trusting **us** and we will be honoring and respecting Them in far greater measure!

God planted that very desire in my heart decades ago for His purposes and obviously **now I see** the enemy did not want me to comprehend and utilize what and who we are **in Christ!** Oh precious Readers, let us blaze forward from our seated in a Heavenly position **now** and keep growing into greater maturity, Heb. 13:20-22 so we accomplish what God has foreordained specifically for us, as we are constantly being changed into the image of Christ. Rom. 8:29

Father God really deeply desires to share in **every** single aspect of our lives whether **we** consider it to be of great importance or not, because He yearns for **continual** fellowship. One thing which delights my heart is to watch and listen to Almighty God's animals, especially birds, because of their infinite variety in songs, actions, sizes and colors. So I have six or seven feeders, bird baths and attractions in our back yard. Indoors we have one wall wallpapered with humming birds, as well as two singing bird clocks. Rather than instinct I really believe birds are eager to obey! Do you recall how heaps of fish must have obeyed the Words of Jesus, when they overloaded Peter's nets, after he obeyed? John 21:5-6

One day years ago, as I was hanging up my laundry, a wee hummingbird came hovering above my right hand. Can you guess why? It must have thought my pearl ring was an interesting insect. I'm enchanted by such adventures. By the way after that event my ring was missing, following a game of badminton with the children. We looked diligently in the grass on our hands and knees but to no avail. However, I had learned to ask God for an angel to protect my belongings, to shine a light on hidden things or cause them to be visible!

**Months later** when I'd forgotten about it, I was changing the sheets on one of the beds and in the corner of a fitted sheet nestled the ring — a **treasure** which had been purchased and given to me on our third anniversary when John and I were in Japan. It reminded me of one of the descriptions of the Kingdom of heaven told by our Lord Jesus, a precious "pearl of great price." He said, "45Again, the kingdom of heaven is like a travelling merchant-buyer seeking beautiful pearls; 46and having found one pearl of great value, having gone off, sold all, as much as he was possessing, having staked all that he had in one business venture which would either make or break him, and purchased it in the market place." Matt. 13 Wuest

It was valuable enough to God, I believe, because it honored our covenant marriage, reflecting back to esteeming His covenant with His **first-born** Son, Jesus, **His** Pearl of Great Price. Do we value this perfect covenant in order to see more clearly spiritually from **God's** eyes and understand His **heart?** As a result of this revelation you will honor and respect **human beings** more deeply, as well as animals, flowers, waterfalls, mountains, stars, even sand. You will see clearly why you devalue **no one** made in the image of God, anyone who has chosen to follow Jesus. Mark 2:14 Instead compassion is released in immeasurable degrees from deep within our spirits. Don't **we** become that "pearl of great price" Matt. 13:46 because Jesus is our Head and we are His Body corporately? Eph. 1:22-23

Did you notice I mentioned sand in the last paragraph above? Why on earth? Because shortly after I was Baptized in the Holy Spirit, our family was vacationing at Honeyman Park in the state of Oregon, where there are beautiful and **bounteous** golden orange sand dunes. As we were riding down a very steep one in a dune buggy, the Holy Spirit asked if I recalled what God had told Abraham, regarding **sand** in Genesis. In 22:17, "in blessing I will bless you, and in multiplying I will multiply your descendants as the stars of the heaven and as the sand which *is* on the seashore; and your descendants shall possess the gate of their enemies." I did and looking, trying to imagine each grain, I was utterly astounded as I pondered those mountainous sand dunes, so many in **one** location! Even with millions of people being redeemed these days it is still more than I can comprehend. But Almighty God is unable to lie!

In Matthew 13:16 Wuest translates that the disciples' eyes and ears are "spiritually prosperous" because they **see** and **hear** and **ours** are the same, because they perceive the meanings hidden within the parables Jesus shared! In other words we are to read by and with the Holy Spirit! This really thrills me that God entrusts **His** sons and daughters with hidden meanings, concealed from others to enrich our lives, Mark 4:11 and that many mysteries in both the Old and New Testaments which have been kept secret for hundreds and hundreds of years are unfolding these days. Promises He made are constantly being exposed and revelations in the established Word, showing so much about the faithfulness and Truth of Daddy God. The rubble of past misunderstandings is being swept away! Don't you just **worship, exalt** and **adore Him!** We are so **Blessed** to have been born for such a time as this. Esther 4:14

# CHAPTER 15

## Search the Scriptures Like a Treasure Digger and a Bounty Hunter

As I related in my first book *The Victor's Mind Can Be Yours*, I really did **ask** and **search** for a prayer partner, but Almighty God had even **more** in mind! He knew the next step for me was to be personally discipled, so I'd follow Jesus more closely! No place in the Bible is the command to "follow Me" (Jesus) rescinded, Matt. 16:24 so we know Him through the Written Word by studying and following what He **said** and **did.** Since Ethel's calling was the office of a prophet and teacher, for me to be trained for the same calling was essential but neither one of us knew that at the start. Ethel was directed to disciple me, as had been done years before for her, but I was noisy with a personality quite opposite to hers, so for that reason, probably more, she wanted nothing to do with me, **but** she **obeyed** Almighty God!

For my sake it's a good thing she knew the verse: "And to love Him (God) with all the heart, with all the understanding, with all the soul, and with all the strength, and to love one's neighbor as oneself, is more than all the whole burnt offerings and sacrifices." Mark 12:33; 1 Sam. 15:22 I'm forever grateful both eternally and daily that she did, for I surely was spiritually deficient and emotionally off balance. We do truly need to realize the **heart** desire of God is **for us,** who willingly and dearly love to follow Him, to be **changed** into the **image** of His dear Son,

**Jesus,** so He could "be the firstborn among many brethren." Rom. 8:28-29 Glory to God!

I was definitely an **unpolished** jewel, but together we delved into the Word and prayer, and **grew** in different ways and were scrumptiously delighted one day when we found this golden nugget in Malachi 3. AMP "16Then those who feared the Lord talked often one to another; and the Lord listened and heard it, and a book of remembrance was written before Him of those who reverenced *and* worshipfully feared the Lord, and who thought on His name. 17'And they shall be Mine,' says the Lord of hosts, 'in that day when I publicly recognize *and* openly declare them to be My jewels — My special possession, My peculiar treasure. And I will spare them, as a man spares his own son who serves him.' "

I suspect many more events, probably all valuable in God's sight, are recorded for eternity in **myriads** of books in Heaven. I've read of trustworthy Christians, numbering **six** or even **seven,** who have literally visited Heaven where they saw many books in which episodes of some kind have been **diligently** and **accurately** written. Though we surely do **not** base any Scriptures on people's experiences, nevertheless **experiences** can often indisputably and helpfully **reinforce** and **establish** the Scriptures inside us! I believe there are countless books there because of *The Lamb's Book of Life* Rev. 20:12 and other books mentioned throughout the Scriptures.

**Most** importantly everything that Jesus accomplished was never even recorded on **earth** but certainly every single event is recorded in Heaven, because He always glorified Father God! John 21:25, "And there are also many other things that Jesus did, which if they were written one by one, I suppose that even the world itself could not contain the books that would be written. Amen." As He spoke **only**

what Father God spoke to Him, His words could **not** fall to the ground! Also, see Psalm 139:16 and Daniel 7:10. Awesome!

What do **you** think might be in books written about us? Truth about our lives including our **idle words** said, Matt. 12:36 let's ask God for a crop failure on these with withered roots or uprooted, rewards for actions which pleased God, and gifts we've given? Many things here on earth are reflections of what we will find in Heaven, so as there are mansions, John 14:2 gazebos, animals, rainbows, rivers, gorgeous flowers, waterfalls, mountains, trees, fish and on and on, there are **many** books!

We were into deliverances of individuals, **removing burdens and destroying yokes of bondage** Isa. 10:27 only by the Holy Spirit's leading with abundant revelations, plus we were blessed with **many** answers to agreement prayers! However, we did not know the changes and fullness of what Almighty God through His Holy Spirit was accomplishing until months passed. One day my daughter, Suzanna, had an appendix attack and although she went to the hospital, it was a **very** brief incident because she agreed with what Ethel and I had prayed. Combining her faith with ours, she came home quickly with **no operation** required!

This really let us appreciate from our experience the value of the **agreement** prayer in **reality** in Matthew 18:19, "Again I say to you that if two of you agree on earth concerning anything that they ask, it will be done for them by My Father in Heaven." Al Houghton's book entitled *The Power of Agreement* was an immense blessing! We had established in prayer that she definitely did not need a knife cutting into her, as we were **totally** trusting in Almighty God and following Proverbs 4:20-23.

Such wonderful life changes thrilled our hearts, because Jesus came to **restore** all things Matt. 12:13; Mark 8:25; Joel 2:25 AMP and also to plant and release His **joy.** We knew we were doing as our Father had commanded and we're longing to be doing even greater works than He did, as Jesus had said we would! John 14:12, AMP "I assure you, most solemnly I tell you, if any one steadfastly believes in Me, he will himself be able to do the things that I do; and he will do even greater things than these, because I go to the Father."

You know since Father God refers to us as sheep, John 10 I recently **saw** a flock of sheep, having just been sheared who were quickly released from a barn after having been cooped up all day. When that door flew open some were running with great gusto, while others were jumping straight up from all fours exuding great joy! Yes, let's finish our race with **exuberant** joy! Acts 20:24 says what I really want to do! How about you?

Almost instantly when I became saturated with the Holy Spirit, I began receiving the gifts of words of knowledge, wisdom, prophecy and discerning of spirits. 1 Corinth. 12:8-10 Also I was led to study about the **Blood** at this time, even giving prophecies to the Body of Christ at churches and to individuals regarding the **Blood** of Jesus. It became my **song** literally and figuratively (probably will continue until I graduate to Heaven!) and in decrees, declarations and prophecies, regarding **Its value** to the Body of Christ in every gathering I attended! This was so enjoyable because so many extra meetings were being held locally at that time. What a privilege!

For an extended period then churches were flooded also with the gifts of the Spirit. There was a wide-spread number of visiting pastors inundating our area from other cities and states, visiting different churches in the area to bring enriched messages from the Bible with signs and wonders following in profusion! Mark 16:20 But at the same time the prophecies, given by us in many places I attended, were not necessarily taken to heart nor handled as wisely as they are now; for I believe the Body of Christ was in the learning process.

But by the same token many churches squelched or grieved the Holy Spirit, partially by failing to trust Him in and through others.

Frequently learning requires mistakes, but many leaders were unwilling or inexperienced in handling the mistakes in love. More light was being revealed to the Body of Christ at that time, too! Today we know God is speaking revelations often and in many ways through the Written Word, through our sons and daughters, angels, visions, illustrations, "ideas, concepts, insights" and dreams! Acts 2:17-18 **Knowledge now** abounds lavishly and is increasing almost as rapidly as we blink our eyes. Glory is here! Though many of our churches have **not yet** freed the Holy Spirit by trusting Him, **it will happen!**

Increasing hunger was so strong then, I often attended **many** home and church meetings for months. This hunger is being rekindled in these days, also! A unity in the Holy Spirit began because of a pervasive appetite, so we were often invited to homes of strangers several nights each week for it was **all** that many of us longed to do, like the first church. Acts 2:46-47 Consequently, we were saturating ourselves in the Holy Spirit, in the Written Word and in fellowship with the Body of Christ. Excitement poured like a cascade of rain.

Almighty God initiated the Blood Covenant in the Biblical books of Genesis through Revelation. As God was moving so specially, teaching about the Blood Covenant burst forth in many Christian meetings. This is so foundational and extensive in the Bible, that if one studies the **great** magnitude of it, a **bonus** of **understanding** the Word in greater measure is the result! Faith for oneself and others becomes so deeply implanted that believing, receiving and grabbing your inheritance is like opening an enormous quantity of surprise packages instantly. If one's understanding is lacking regarding Blood Covenant it is most difficult to comprehend the Holy Bible in clarity and depth, as a Living Book, really seeing God's *agapé* love and plan, as well as His matchless wisdom and knowledge. It is almost unquestionably impossible.

Often I believe our Father gives such a **fervent song** assignment as our calling Eph. 1:18; 4:1 that it seems overwhelming to others at times, but we are to stay faithful to what He has commanded, until He leads us to other pathways! We become almost like **specialists** in one portion of the Bible, yet we never can exhaust even one verse!

Because of being involved in many demonic deliverances so quickly after receiving the Baptism in the Holy Spirit, Acts 2:1-4 I believe in **retrospect** the **wisdom** of God **protected** me mightily from getting lopsided or deceived, due to studying the Blood at the same time. For human beings can tend to concentrate so fully on one thing, they can tilt, hit a wall or get off balance into one ditch or the other, unless they stay on guard!

As I grew I was asked and led to co-head a women's group meeting held once monthly at a near-by restaurant with a younger woman, Becky, which surely expanded His ministry through me. It demanded much more prayer, **acute** listening to others, resulting in developing more direction, compassion, plus understanding and knowledge. He revealed to us whom He desired to be the speaker and we just did the interim business for the most part! We often ministered at the end though and then those who wanted to eat did so afterwards, for we met in a good-sized room at the restaurant. This was how we became more acquainted than just "hello and good-bye."

One month I was asked to speak and I remember when searching for a subject, the Holy Spirit directed me to reach inside my washing machine between the inner and outer tub, where I found a dingy colored, ugly worn sock. The supposedly **white** sock had very gray streaks, (obviously it had been there for a while), just as our sins keep darkness inside, unless we keep a squeaky clean heart and spirit through immediate repentance and total **eradication** by His Blood! 1 John 1:9 This is a complete cleansing, more than a mere atonement as in the Old Testament. Father God said, **"Take that sock and a white clean matching one and use it for an illustration."**

Then the Holy Spirit directed me to the Scripture in Matthew 21:12-13, AMP where Jesus had driven out the buyers and sellers in the temple! He reprimanded them in righteous anger, saying "13The Scripture says, My house shall be called a house of prayer; but you have made it a den of robbers." He revealed that each of us is **not** only the **temple** of the Holy Spirit 1 Corinth. 6:19 but that we are to be a **house** of **prayer** also! Scripture does command us to pray without ceasing and perseveringly. 1 Thess. 5:17 AMP It's encouraging to remember that prayer is talking to and listening to God!

One reason I'm led to include these incidents is to reveal how God leads us to follow **closely His** pathway individually designed for us, according to the Scriptures, when we're allowing Him to be Lord. I've heard it said "If He is not Lord of all, He is not Lord at all." It truly is a process, but the realization can strike us like a streak of lightning. Do you recall Saul's (later renamed Paul) remark on the road to Damascus? When he encountered the Living God he said "Who are You, Lord?" Acts 9:5 He surely recognized Him but also, I believe was immediately struck that **He is Lord!**

Another dynamic incident happened in the late 1970's, when one Sunday at church, the Pastor motioned for me to minister to a woman there for salvation, which I did. In the afternoon I went to the hospital, where my Mom had been in a coma for several days, as she was being given 100% oxygen, getting ready to **graduate** to Heaven but **unable** to leave earth. Mother had said earlier "Mary, it is hard to die!" But Abba Father had a reason to keep her here, revealed to Ethel who had been praying at home, and joined me later at the hospital where she asked, "Has your Mom ever said Jesus is **Lord?**" After a thoughtful moment I said, "I don't think so, though I know she believes He was raised from the dead." She went over to the bed and said "Margaret can you say, Jesus is Lord? " At this point Mom could only **babble** syllables, but she looked **right** in Ethel's eyes and said something like, "**Ouas** eea ehh **ord!**" Twelve hours later she **graduated** to Heaven!

Now I was **very** impressed by the Scripture, Romans 10:9-10, which Ethel had received, as I realized God kept Mom on earth until **she made** the declaration. The doctors couldn't understand **what** was keeping her here, because she was seventy-nine years old with many health problems and the coma had lasted five days with no feeding. I saw the tenderness, mercy and protection of Daddy God so strongly in this situation, that I phoned the woman I'd met at the altar and had her say Romans 10:9-10. AMP "9Because if you acknowledge *and* confess with your lips that Jesus is Lord and in your heart believe (adhere to, trust in and rely on the truth) that God raised Him from the dead, you will be saved. 10For with the heart a person believe (adhere to, trust in and rely on Christ) and so is justified (declared righteous, acceptable to God), and with the mouth he confesses — declares openly and speaks out freely his faith — *and* confirms [his] salvation."

Later one of the women in my prayer group accused me of being legalistic, but Our God is a perfect **Lawgiver** and He requires that we are accurate in our obeying the Scriptures. When things are not precise and clear then there are no absolutes, and dreadful confusion abounds. For example once in the 1970's, I heard a pastor say that when we stopped teaching about Heaven and hell as **real** locations, boundaries disappeared, and many people began to push God away, by **ignoring, denying, neglecting** or **rebelling against** Him!

God corrected me once in 1988, immediately after Ethel went to Heaven, explaining only our **body suit dies,** but **not** our **spirit** nor our **soul,** for we are eternal beings, 1 Corinth. 15 thus going to Heaven with Jehovah God, Jesus and the Holy Spirit or to hell with Satan and his cohorts. He used Numbers 13 and 14, where He had told Moses Canaan **was theirs,** but he was to send twelve spies with specific instructions and they were commanded to "be of good courage!" 13:20 But ten gave fearful, "evil" 13:32 AMP reports and because they saw the people as giants and called **themselves** "grasshoppers," 13:33 AMP they **convinced themselves** and **believed** they were seen by the people in the same way. Almighty God had given them **positive directions prior** to spying, which they should have kept in their hearts and minds, **disregarding** what others **said! So must we!**

So in my case, when I was asked to tell the Pastor locally, God said I was to say **"Ethel has graduated to Heaven not died because she was not dead."** He said **for me** to declare otherwise **"would be an evil report."** Since then I am not to send cards at such times with the word **"sympathy"** to anyone, because it does not bring **"life."** The Holy Spirit, the Comforter, brings life in His **"comfort!"**

There are definite warnings from God in the Bible to remember **Who** has brought us out of **Egypt** (mistakes, bad choices, damaging habits such as living by our **senses,** which are so **fickle** and much more). Deuteronomy 6:12 People who don't know Him cannot appreciate how He must feel, **yes, feel,** when He created us to be in His large family, has given us freedom to choose or neglect Him and we do much worse! We **reject Him** Who **is** our Life and Who has given us life and knows us completely inside-out, desiring and providing only **His best** for our lives!

However, today things are changing and Heaven and hell are being proclaimed once more in conjunction with the Bible as **real eternal** locations. Recognize, Honor and Respect our Magnificent Creator, Savior Redeemer and returning King! Surely the **only** true living God, our Creator, ought to know what is the most worth-while plan for our lives!

# CHAPTER 16

## Snatching the Prize!

In my youthful years before teens and a little beyond, I had a neighborhood friend, Shirley, an only daughter, who lived about a block away! She and I got along very well, can't ever recall being angry with her at all. Her parents were very good to me, even asked if I could go with them to Lake Okoboji, Iowa one summer on their vacation. They had a car, which sat only two inside, with a rumble seat, so we could make noise, sing, talk, laugh and they were separated from our uproar. (Some of you dearly Beloved Readers may not know what a rumble seat was. It was a folding seat for two located in the back of an automobile, where the trunk in many cars would be today.)

At the very back of us was where we roped our luggage onto a rack and off we'd go. It was another peaceful breather for me from my parents fighting at home, because her parents were at peace with one another, humble, kind, and enjoyed each other and whatever happened in life.

On the trip, Mr. Hudson's cigarette or a spark must have landed on our luggage, because it caught on fire. Shirley and I were having so much fun we were totally oblivious to it, but another driver caught Mr. Hudson's attention. Abruptly we halted and scrambled up a hill by the road. I grabbed my suitcase first, losing nothing. As I recall I think mine was one of the top suitcases. They were proud I had the presence of mind to get it and thankfully they also lost very little.

At the lake we played some simple games with foam, shells and dead fish and we swam in rain or shine! We also were given some money, about a dollar apiece occasionally, to go to a near-by, small and simplistic recreational park with rides such as a merry-go-round, a roller coaster, small bumper cars and a few others. At the **end** of each complete ride on the merry-go-round there was a very **grandiose lion statue** that dispensed silver rings, which we tried to snatch one at a time from his partially open mouth! **If** we were up in the air high enough as we rode by on our horse, the final ring — a **golden** one — won a **free** ride for whoever grabbed it. So we would get there early and since we were alone on the ride, one or the other eventually caught the golden one. Consequently you can see we had a uniquely enjoyable time with **no** competition and our money went a long way. Naturally we had fewer trips later as the park got busier!

Now I've come to know Jesus our "Lion of the tribe of Judah," Rev. 5:5 and our "adversary the devil" who "walks about like a roaring lion, seeking whom he may devour," 1 Pet. 5:8 that big golden lion has come to represent much more in my heart symbolically and literally. It reminds me of C.S. Lewis's Aslan in his *Narnia* book series. We are "more than conquerors," Rom. 8:37 victorious in our spiritual walk and like Jesus we can release a roar that **scares** the devil clear out of our lives, 1 John 4:4 as well as release genuinely loud laughter.

I can remember having a real desire to see that **statue** not just for the ring, yet was unable **then** to see the significance. The **golden** ring now symbolizes to me **victory** in every area of our lives eternally, purchased by the Blood and work of our precious Lord on the Cross and in hell, when all the principalities, powers, rulers of darkness, and wicked spirits in heavenly places were defeated. Eph. 6:12; Col. 2:15 Our **Lord, High Priest** and **soon coming King** legally captured and now possesses the **keys** of death, hell and the grave. Rev. 1:18 Alleluia! **Maranatha!**

———⊗⊗⊗———

# CHAPTER 17

# Introduction to Applying His Blood

Now it seems we are at a place to reveal some of the magnificence in utilizing the **Blood** and applying It as a **tool** of Victory. It is so totally amazing. Because It is still **alive, speaks** Heb. 12:24 and is so **powerful** It can accomplish **far more** than you or I can imagine or think. But first of all, there is one verse Father God revealed to my heart a number of years ago that I had to read many times, thinking I must be reading it amiss. Truly because of our **individual** callings or commandments by Almighty God, it seems to me the Holy Spirit **can reveal** and **emphasize** different aspects of a Scripture, resulting in it being incredibly **pregnant** with many thoughts and still not be in error, as long as they are Holy Spirit **inspired.**

Sometimes the understanding is applied by God so **individually** and **uniquely** it is **not** always applicable to someone else. It is rather similar to viewing a mountain from one side and then next time seeing it from another, and realizing it is very dissimilar. This is why I think when we get to Heaven to get our resurrected bodies, our home, Rom. 8:22; 2 Corinth. 5:6 we will continue learning for eternity, because we never can exhaust God's love, wisdom, creative ideas and actions, understanding, knowledge, justice, abilities or anything else in any way!

Here is the Scripture to which I refer with a meaningful, dependent and descriptive clause — "that great Shepherd of the sheep." Behold

Hebrews 13:20-21. "20Now may the God of peace who brought up our Lord Jesus from the dead, that great Shepherd of the sheep, through the Blood of the everlasting covenant, 21make you complete in every good work to do His will, working in you what is well pleasing in His sight, through Jesus Christ, to whom *be* glory forever and ever. Amen."

I include this as a **very basic** Scripture for this and the remaining chapters! Dearly Beloved Reader, meditate as you read the totality in many aspects of the immeasurable dimensions in utilizing our Savior's Blood, for "that great Shepherd of the sheep" could be removed without changing God's meaning. Of great importance here is that the Blood of Jesus will "make you complete" or as the Greek says **"adjusts you,"** while Wuest's translation says It will "equip you in every good thing (work) to do His (God's) will." To me this means **honor** and **respect** It, as you are to apply It, plead It at appropriate times, and never forget that **It is anointed, alive, powerful** and **speaking** of **Jesus,** His love, mercy, grace, forgiveness and the Written Word. Also, to believe the truth of the various usages should any be new to you, please consult and listen to our Teacher, the Holy Spirit, and His "stop or go."

Let us enrich our understanding of the infinite value of our physical blood **more,** which is "a fixed tissue" not just a liquid but "fluid and mobile," so "it is free to move throughout the entire body, and supply the fixed cells with nourishment and carry off the waste products and the 'ashes' of cell activity. In the normal human body there are about five quarts of this fluid, and this blood pumped by the heart circulates through the system about every twenty-three seconds, so that every cell in the body is constantly supplied and cleansed and at the same time is in constant communication with every other cell in that body." These facts were gleaned from *The Chemistry of the Blood pg 14* by M.R. DeHaan, M.D. It is one of the **mysteries** of the Bible to me, for it is almost comparable to having a filthy garbage truck changing into a spotless "meals on wheels" truck in **twenty-three seconds!** Our Creator, God, is totally awesome and good beyond measure.

Since Father God led me to complete, especially in the 1980s, almost three hundred spiritual home and business **blessings,** I have been applying **It** and pleading **It** for decades in a great **variety** of situations. Some applications may seem most unusual, but many instant results were astounding! Naturally I'm unable to include **all** of them but some **may** be unique and release **new** insights or **confirm** your need to make changes or **apply** the Blood to stamp out undesirable situations, as you grow in understanding.

How this was instigated is a mystery, because I usually simply listen to do the **next** thing God tells me to do without my long range plan, unless He has initiated one, such as this book. But in the early days of being discipled by Ethel, we often prayed for people who came to us. Among other things the Holy Spirit would frequently reveal various evil spirits **harassing** them, so we obviously willingly set them free Mark 16:17-20 in Jesus! John 14:12-14

These evil spirits in **former** years have often been evidenced far more in third world countries. But as the world is getting smaller because of easier travel, countless people are entering the United States from various countries with evil spirits accompanying a number of them. Also, as prophesied in these last days the **darkness** is increasing rapidly, Isa. 60:1-3 resulting in ignorance regarding the Living God or ugly rebellion against Him by worshipping false gods! Today the "gods" worshipped can be that of oppressive power over others, physical abuse, sex, nudity, or varied perverseness, recreation of all kinds, nature, and on and on goes the list.

Thanks be to our Precious God His glory is shining far **brighter** outweighing the evil! But the enemy and cohorts' task is still the same — hassling, deceiving, perverting and poisoning the minds and emotions of children, teen-agers and adults! In fact, if they can cause **you** to believe that the Written Word is not going to accomplish what it says for **you,** the enemy can **deceive** you in your mind, making you accept **defeat.**

Think of how many trials Paul endured to **verify** the Blood Covenant, 2 Corinth. 11:23-28 yet God delivered him out of every one! 2 Tim. 3:11 Then, as a **victor** he could write Romans 8:35-37. "35Who shall separate us from the love of Christ? *Shall* tribulation, or distress, or persecution, or famine, or nakedness, or peril, or sword? 36As it is written: 'For Your sake we are killed all day long; we are accounted as sheep for the slaughter.' 37Yet in all these things we are more than conquerors through Him who loved us."

Also, sometimes a person would mention an unusual thing happening in some part of their garage, attic, closets, hidden spaces, fireplaces or other areas in the home. This gradually led to our seeking and uncovering more of the devil's antics, so it led to my **Blessing** them through **spiritual** house cleanings. Josh. 7:11-13 Also, one day I was just talking to God and there I had a brief vision of a huge V-shaped cloud of dark creatures flying rapidly. When I asked God "What on earth does that mean?" He replied **"Those are grief spirits, which will be loosed in the last days to plague My people!"** Luke 21:25-26

Another vision which came about this time was of a broad ramp, cattle-sized, at the top of which was a huge Dutch door, the bottom restraining many **vacant-eyed** people. Later, I believe this was revealed as a vision of people, who would be helped through what God directed me to do, **if** I willingly obeyed His commands. Isa. 61:1-3 Much, much earlier He had drawn my attention to a fire thorn bush with hundreds of berries, which dragged the branches to the ground in a churchyard where I was praying. He said **"I will make you as fruitful as that bush if you follow and obey Me!"** John 15:5

Because I was also studying about the **Blood** and increasing in understanding Its power and the Word of God along with these activities, more and more people asked and detected things in their homes, which they had **tolerated, underrated** or tried to **ignore** but which were weird, uncomfortable, unfamiliar or even had a strange odor, such as sulfur!

Until this time the people developed patterns of avoidance, sometimes apprehension or had not consciously really considered the situation seriously, so certain rooms or areas became verboten. Consequently Almighty God gave me a check list to share (see chapter end) and directed me to **train** the Christians, who were interested, with a number of things they could do, as well as listen to an instructive tape to help prior to the cleansing and blessing!

Later as more and more people wanted us to come, in the church I was attending, I was invited to teach two classes during a conference, lasting several days with a number of apostles, pastors and teachers in the Body of Christ. One of the pastors asked me to come to teach at his church for a Saturday seminar! Also, so many questions were springing up, I held a one day seminar to **train** more people, so they could spiritually clean and bless their own homes, leaving me to go only to the more **difficult** situations, because of time limitation. On one occasion for Women's **Aglow** it was a huge privilege to be able to teach several classes on the same subjects for a week-end seminar in Port Townsend.

Once there was a one day teaching in Port Orchard, where I was led to prophesy to **every** person present. Lo and behold, the hostess showed me pictures on the wall of her four children for individual prophecies. When I returned to the living room, snapshots of all the women's children were lying on the table for their words! At another time when invited to a home meeting, God had not given me any message, but when I arrived every woman had a tape recorder to receive her word, which she did. What a transfiguring and encouraging difference resulted every time, and often peace greatly increased between family members! Delightful fullness of joy permeated the atmosphere! To God be the Glory and thank You Lord for the fun! Quite a deviation from tromping on the enemy.

Returning to the house blessings, some of the **first** things God revealed, as we went from room to room, were hidden objects or forgotten ones in boxes, storage places, even fireplaces, on shelves in closets, in basements or attics. It was truly amazing and never the same twice. Other things were valued even as curiosities, carved masks, totem pole replicas, "treasures" or gifts purchased at import stores or in foreign countries — objects of worship, statues, unusual art objects from other cultures and religions. Some had even been prayed over in the countries of their origin for enticing and seducing spirits to **accompany** the objects to produce **harmful** results!

Many people **do not realize** that Satan is such an insidious and deadly legalist as well as an opportunist, especially if ignored! He believes he can demand his cohorts to enter homes or hover around to harass people who have stored papers, pictures, rings, or other objects **possibly** used or connected with ceremonies where demonic influences reigned! Acts 19:19 His pride is worn like a cloak and his twisted, ugly, constant desire is to discredit and bring lying doubts against God and His Word and then occupy persons with his **black** hatred, Matt. 12:43-45 so he can take them to **hell.**

Also, demons delight in Satan's command to speak to people through **their** objects and idols to gain their worship. They are fully aware that the time is here when "23the true (genuine) worshippers will worship the Father in spirit and in truth (reality); for the Father is seeking just such people as these as His worshippers. 24God is a Spirit (a spiritual Being) and those who worship Him must worship *Him* in spirit and in truth (reality)." John 4 AMP In the Old Testament many had altars built on high places, where sacrifices were offered to demons. Lev. 17:7; 1 Kings 14:23 We are to **focus** on **Jesus,** our **power** and **authority** over them Luke 10:19 AMP and their cruel "wiles" Eph. 6:11 plus their intentions. Let's always remain alert, and not be ignorant of their devices, 2 Corinth. 2:11 thus maintaining the complete victorious living bought by Jesus and His Blood!

# Maintaining Victory in Jesus in Your Home
## Matthew 12:43-45; Luke 11:24-26; Revelation 3:20

1. Determine and decide in your **will, heart, mind** and **actions** your home is blessed for God's Presence all the time. **Faith reigns as you believe and act on your decision!**

2. Keep **praise** and **worship** flowing!
   *Psalm 148; Psalm 68:3; 1 Chronicles 16:29; 2 Chronicles 20:21*

3. **Speak in tongues** aloud and frequently following the Holy Spirit.
   It will become supernaturally natural after a while.
   *Ephesians 6:18; 1 Corinthians 14:4*

4. **Know** and **use Jesus' precious Blood** and keep understanding, declaring and decreeing the value of the **Blood Covenant** to your family.
   *Revelation 12:11; Exodus 12*

5. Know who **you are in Jesus!**
   *Romans 8:3* as well as many, many other Scriptures

6. Deepen your knowledge and use of the **Name of Jesus and His Blood** as you continually listen to the Holy Spirit.

7. Keep loosing **spiritual authority** and **God's anointing** through you into your home.
   Keep on keeping on, releasing spiritual authority. Tromp on doubt and unbelief!

8. Consciously **guard against** fear, arguments, strife, dissension, foul attitudes and quarreling.
   These open the door for further enemy attacks. **Be earnest, quick repenters. Change!**

9. Keep a **thankful heart** as you continually delight in His Presence.
   *Psalm 50:14; Psalm 116:17*

10. Wear the **armor of God.**
    *Ephesians 6:10-18; Romans 13:12*

11. **Proclaim** loudly, faithfully, and perseveringly what **marvelous victory** has been won after the house blessing.

12. **Stand firm in faith** against the devil so *1 Peter 3:7* and *Matthew 18:18-20* stays a reality.

13. **Do *2 Corinthians 10:3-5* continually, so victory reigns!**

# CHAPTER 18

# Ask Our Wisest Teacher

We need to **remember** the Old Testament people had **no printed Bible** and no true **understanding** of the **enemy** but it is written, "19that which is knowable concerning God is plainly evident in them, for God made it clear to them; 20for the things concerning Him which are invisible since the creation of the universe are clearly seen, being understood by means of the things that are made, namely, His eternal power and divine Being, resulting in their being without a defense. 21Because, knowing God, not as God did they glorify Him, nor were they grateful, but they became futile in their reasonings, and their stupid heart was darkened. 22Asserting themselves to be wise, they became fools 23and exchanged the glory of the incorruptible God for a likeness of an image of corruptible man and of birds and of quadrupeds and of snakes." Rom. 1 Wuest

To me, one of the most outstanding confrontations of God's Kingdom pitted against Satan's in the Old Testament was Elijah confronting **eight hundred** and **fifty** prophets of Asherah and Baal on Mount Carmel. Elijah knew his and our **Living** God, **covenant** and **His authority** and **power!** 1 Kings 18:20-40 David **knew** God and covenant as well even as a young shepherd, 1 Sam. 17: 32-51 as did many other leaders in the Old Testament!

The Holy Spirit reminded me in the New Covenant in the first church in the book of Acts chapter 19 of the open burning of books, owned by those who had **practiced** magic **prior** to being "born again." John 3:3-6 They changed their thinking **very** quickly after they realized they had been following Satan and in their hearts they decided to **honor** and **respect** Almighty God pronto! Many believers today, Beloved, need to examine themselves and their homes, so strife and conflict can be permanently stamped out. Father God told me once, **"You do not have to deliver people privately because Satan does hidden works in darkness. I don't!"** Truly I believe it is no longer the time to be **under-cover** or **silent** about our exciting Lord. He actually is the only Person with wisdom, understanding and knowledge Isa. 11:2 to solve every trial, problem, and temptation, James 1:2-5 **if** we willingly obey as faithful **doers** of the Word.

I diligently studied the Old and New Testaments and discovered much about **foreign things,** Deut. 27:15; Judges 10:13-16; Psa. 81:8-10 worshipped and honored, full of power of the enemy, which are **not** to be brought into your home because the enemy can have an entrance into your life. For example see Deuteronomy 7:26. Beloved you can study these Scriptures, too. We do know the Ten Commandments tell us we are not to have any idols, whether figurative or literal. Exod. 20:3-5 What **things** you may be asking? These were things I certainly knew nothing about, until we lived in Japan for fifteen months.

During that time we even discovered and were welcomed to visit a recently built Buddhist temple then, where a woman who helped the priest with the temple was from Tacoma, Washington. The day before there had been over a hundred Buddhist priests at a meeting, but just one when we arrived! The woman even took us into the inner temple, probably the enemy's imitation of the **Holy** of holies part in God's taber-nacle! There was much gold, as well as gaudy red velvet curtains and statues, attempting to imitate the **genuine** grandeur of Heaven of our Almighty Living God. Beloved, do remember Heaven is where he lived before he was cast out. Isa. 14:12-15 He is **never** creative for he can only imitate in a darkened, destructive way.

We took camera shots, but I destroyed many of them after we got home, because they could be an opening for Satan. Besides he is such a legalist and so evil as I've said, he or his underlings can **invade** homes, where they perseveringly wait and watch to cause havoc, resulting in strife and making constant attempts to disturb and **possess** a body. When strife had been active in our family in former years, I've stopped it through **"binding and loosing!"** Matt. 18:18 AMP Also, I've experienced **perverse spirits,** causing others to hear what I did **not** say, so we need to stay alert!

God is **omnipresent** but please know the enemy is **not,** though he dictates orders to his demons to meddle, watch and wait for opportunities to perform his hideous activities, bringing **more** destroyers when we're complacent, allowing things to remain the same. Matt. 12:43-45 God graciously reminded me when we returned from Japan I had bought what I thought **then** to be appealing, **delightful ivory** statues of Japanese **gods.** Yuck! Believe me, when He reminded me they were worshipped, I tried a number of tools to destroy them **immediately,** yet unsuccessfully, so they were taken to the dump.

When three of us went through my home to cleanse and bless it, the **Holy Spirit** revealed a **Mason** covenant paper and ring belonging to John's father hidden with old things under our house. I am so **delighted** to have studied accursed things Josh. 6:18 and am under more **light** than I would have been without so much experience! I've encountered **rival** spirits of error, who support the Masons strongly and I know from personal experience, therefore am "fully persuaded" innocent people have been duped, not realizing what can result from being involved. If some of you are uncertain and I've provoked you, please ask Father God! **Only** Almighty God knows the **extent** of trouble we **avoided** by destroying those belongings. Deut. 7:9 Also, concerning families, many have been seriously damaged Exod. 20:5 who have been ignorant or have rejected the fact that Jesus, also, took **all** generational curses on the Cross! Gal. 3:13-14

One instance was when a team of us was ministering to a woman having serious trouble in her mind, emotions and body, when the Holy Spirit revealed she was wearing a ring, belonging to a former male friend, now married to someone else! She was praying to re-establish a **close** relationship with him. She would **not** get rid of it at that time, consequently we could not assist her in any way! We can surely change many thorny circumstances by being wise about all Jesus accomplished and being **willing** to obey, **believe, listen** and **trust** God whether we **understand** or not!

However, God does make something crystal clear throughout the Bible! He **honors marriages,** because He desires to be in **covenant** with a man and woman in order to restore a **sacred, beautiful,** growing in depth, enduring relationship with this couple in His family of Love! We learn in biology a woman has a hymen membrane, originally a sign of a virgin and **blood covenant** with her husband and God, partially covering her vagina to be penetrated in the **marriage** act. All of this is on such a highly cherished level, few know or realize how desecrated it has become, when people act so **far** beneath God's desire for their good! He gave sex as a precious **gift** for **marriage** when respected and honored His way!

Several couples shared the union even becomes another weapon in spiritual **warfare! God revealed** to me, because **He** is present the enemy is shut out, the covenant is strengthened and the enjoyment is increased. Do you see why the enemy works so wickedly to **destroy** wholesome and pure marriages? This is **God's perfect** and **healthy** design for spirit, soul and body. No wonder it can produce **life,** a privilege. **He** receives much **Glory** and **joyfulness** from **this!**

Whenever we decide **against His way** however, we jeopardize our very lives, truth, health, joy, purity, loveliness, beauty, justice, honesty and on and on. Why on earth am I saying this? Beloved, the plan was perfect, but when **experimenting** occurs with the sacred sex act, for example, individuals are **prime** targets for wicked spirits, because their **souls** are connecting in lust **momentarily!** At that second our arch enemy can bring **many** evil spirits, such as perverse, error, grief, fear, destruction, depression, suicide and on and on, who are looking for a permanent home. They can bring extreme terror to your mind forever, day and night. Please study and hear Isaiah 50:10-11. AMP Every addiction has its own **hideous** and **destructive** swarm of spirits, some more powerful than others, who are deceptive, and can regroup and yearn to take you to hell. But we have the help and protection of angels!

Would you build a house, put in the electricity, plumbing, flooring, perhaps with just your ideas of the moment, not based on **sound** judgment? You might as well build a sand castle on the ocean beach for neither will be successful at all. Almighty God, our Creator **trusted us** with free wills. **Only He** knows what is the **very** finest, pure and **completely** enjoyable life and how to live it!

One more thing, I doubt if anyone thoroughly understands all the insidious tricks the enemy has utilized to deceive and infect many, many lives, particularly pertaining to preventing persons from being **Born Again** or totally misrepresenting God. He **is** perfect Love, not a **hard task master** Whom they need to fear when mistakes are made. Matt. 11:28-30 In fact, I know several persons to whom God has said, **"You're harder on people than I am!"** Satan even accuses Almighty God of being the killer, when in actuality he is, while our **Lord God** is always demonstrating **enduring** love and **constant** protection in our lives! Unbelievers, when going down our enemy's path, if they fail to **repent** will draw the wrath of God due to the law of sin and evil, resulting in death. Rom. 8:1-2 Please know God and Satan are **not** opposites **nor equal** in any way, as he was created by God but because of his pride, **he** chose evil.

Another attribute in many people is **great** intelligence, which can be difficult when reading the Bible, especially revealed to me decades ago, because I've been **led** (confirmed by a mature prophet and teacher in the Body of Christ) to minister to a number of them. Many times these people **think** they must acquire **understanding before** they proceed following any directions from Almighty God, and have practiced their faith muscles for awhile. Faith does lead us to understanding but progressively as we delve into the Written Word!

Also, because of such a gift from God, it is often most difficult to **cease** trying to figure things out, Prov. 3:5-6 abdicate or release logic or man's reasoning Rom 12:2 and **accept** praying in tongues from our Baptizer, Precious Jesus! You see, worldly education not based on the Bible develops and rewards intelligence. What is truly needed is common sense **inside** us added to the Word, asking and allowing the Holy Spirit to teach us in our spirit! Once Daddy God gave me **"sanctified common sense"** for that way it's stamped and approved by Him.

Our Lord Jesus followed His Father diligently and wholly, Mark 14:36; John 14:10-11 so when we have a relationship with Jesus, **He** will then **introduce** us to "Abba" Father God. Be certain, Dear Reader, to **meet Him,** so **you** can know deep Love John 17:21 26 AMP and release True, Pure Love from the Holy Spirit within you, Rom. 5:5 attracting others to know Jesus. "15For we are the sweet fragrance of Christ [which exhales] unto God." 2 Corinth. 2:14-16 AMP Remember you are inseparably integrated in union, I call it **homogenized** with Father, Son and Holy Spirit, the second you accept Jesus as Lord and Savior! John 14:20-21

# CHAPTER 19

# Continue Applying His Living Blood

Some people delivered from Satan's feeble attempts to destroy God's Gift of health have told **true** events of God's miracles. So I'll touch on **some** unusual incidents in our lives. Tighten your seat belts for His truth can surprise you. Let's start at the beginning of life itself; I've **declared** and **decreed** protection of the Blood in the union of husbands and wives over their sperms and eggs, for the conception of a **healthy** baby in every way — spirit, soul and body. Also, I've been led to pray protection of the womb itself so the embryo would **form** rightly in attaching to the uterus and developing during the pregnancy.

Why? Positively Almighty **God** is **not inadequate** but sin is rampant on the earth. Satan has atrociously in sneaky and subtle ways wormed into circumstances, if we are **unaware** or **lax** in **keeping faith** muscles alive and declaring Scriptures! Failing to hear His Spirit in ours, it **is** possible to fall into listening to what our senses are telling us or wild stories other than God's **Truth!** Since **Bible hope** means **"eager expectancy"** you will not swallow enemy lies if you are established in His Word. Heb. 4:12 Besides we can speak careless and idle words, failing to know or understand words are containers. We have tremendous authority from Jesus when we speak, whether wisely or unwisely! Beloved, please keep in mind my assignment from God is to assist you in preventing, whenever possible, the destruction the enemy would viciously enjoy doing! Do remember he is the enemy to Christians!

Also, parents-to-be can swallow tales from their own upbringing or other married people, which can plant **wrong** seeds in their thinking, therefore bearing polluted fruit. Wholly realize the value in our Heavenly Father's heart regarding **Life** and the precious way the Holy Spirit expressed it through David in Psalm 139 starting with "13For You did form my inward parts, You did knit me together in my mother's womb. 14I will confess *and* praise You, for You are fearfully wonderful, *and* for the awful wonder of my birth! Wonderful are Your works, and that my inner self knows right well. 15My frame was not hidden from You, when I was being formed in secret *and* intricately *and* curiously wrought (as if embroidered with various colors) in the depths of the earth [a region of darkness and mystery]. 16Your eyes saw my unformed substance, and in Your book all the days *of my life* were written, before ever they took shape, when as yet there was none of them." AMP

It's been the leading of the Holy Spirit to pray this way for years for **several** other reasons. Whatever we believe **must be** what the Word says regarding the power of Satan, that he unmistakably **wants** and **will continue trying** "to steal, and to kill, and to destroy." John 10:10 Since we belong either to God or Satan, due to our own choices, if we positively are going to reside in eternity with Almighty God through **receiving Jesus** as **our Lord** and **Savior,** it's vital to know he hates and persistently strives to destroy **us.** Due to his pride and jealousy, he hates God, so he plants suspicion, doubt, deception and evil into **uncircumcised** ears and into **unrenewed** minds! Did you know the Word says we are to have **our hearts, ears** and **lips circumcised** unto God? Start in Acts 7:51 and Exodus 6:30 AMP for understanding.

When this became vital to me, several decades ago, I heard from several Christian sources that there is an identifiable female demon in the Old Testament called Lilith, worshipped by some of the Jewish people in captivity in Babylon, I believe. In Isaiah chapter 34:14 when

God was prophesying the end of Edom, she is clearly mentioned, "Wild cats will meet hyenas there, the satyrs will call to each other, there too will Lilith seek cover taking rest." (Lilith found in a 1983 Thomas Nelson Translation of the New King James Version.) In the American Standard Bible she was referred to as the "night monster." I read that someone had heard from a Jewish source that she was called in their folklore the "Queen of the demons."

Dearly Beloved, I mention this now because we must **protect** our children daily **prior** and **after** their arrival on earth. Why Lilith then? Because she was a night witch who was believed to attack **infants** and **snatch** children. **Several** friends, who were nurses working in hospitals, told me in their experiences at that time, that they definitely observed **crib deaths** happened to **healthy** babies! One nurse even said she believed they were **quickly** choked. We have the **Name** of **Jesus** and His precious **Blood,** His **total** defeat of the enemy — His power and authority — and Psalm 91 to keep our children protected all the time. We can **declare** they each have a guardian angel who sees the face of God in Heaven. Matt. 18:10 We must be on guard and act in God's wisdom and our covenant authority as Victors, certainly **not** in fear. 2 Tim. 1:7 We will walk in faith and trust requiring the Holy Spirit's assistance and perfect awareness, John 16:13 thereby preventing deception, as often as possible. Glory.

One experience displaying God's tenderness and a caring heart was in a home where three young girls lived, one still young enough to sleep in a crib. As I stood there I asked if she jerked when she awoke sometimes. Since the answer was yes, God **very** specifically revealed what to pray, proclaim and declare for her healing. She was healed! In another home the lady had heard noises in her cupboards, whereupon she announced to them "Mary is coming, you'll have to leave!" She had more authority than she realized because by the time we got there, (a team went with me on many of my trips), very little was left to do. Alleluia!

Many times God would give surprising revelation words of knowledge, understanding or wisdom, 1 Corinth. 12:8 which would minister to a circumstance in the marriage of the couple or provide solutions to situations they had prayed about or questioned. Constantly the thanks, glory and honor belong to God, as amazing Blessings poured forth in many ways in **every** single circumstance.

Father God graciously even commenced leaving a sign in the sky, bright sunshine, no matter how the day began weather-wise! It took a while before I realized how precious God was to display His Blessing of approval! The encouragement was immeasurable for the particular task at hand but also acted as a strong green light to continue!

In one cul-de-sac, an acquaintance, whose relative was constructing new homes noticed demonic interferences emerging, so she invited me to come with her to bless each unoccupied home and claim the land as Almighty God's. Between two of the homes there was a generous section of land with a number of trees, forming a circle, where the Holy Spirit revealed a murder had occurred. When we prayed, as the Spirit led, the sun shone suddenly, shining brightly within the circle. Abba Father promised that the ground would be anointed forever. As we Blessed each empty home being built, God would tell us various things to pray. These times were always most exciting and such a Blessing to impart help to the unknown residents, enabling them to partake of God's Blessing.

Other times God revealed there were certain demons of higher power at work, so on occasion revelation came to break their power, since Jesus had already defeated "the rulers of the darkness." Eph. 6; Col. 2:15 Before long the governing city authorities would uncover drugs being manufactured, drug plants being grown, or drug lords discovered where we had prayed and declared. Perhaps God would let us see darkness over homes or He would utter unknown secrets. Frequently, the **gift** of **faith** would inundate the situation, for our trust was easily placed in God, because we **knew nothing** prior to our visits, as I requested from the recipients. Later quite often we would discover the results, when we would spot articles in the newspaper or on the news on TV.

In one home we were listening and declaring, when I glanced in the corner of a dining room and there sat several demons like huge spiders, piggyback, and I heard inaudibly but strongly, "We are legion!" I really laughed and they were instantly gone. Spontaneous joyful laughter does wonders!

Another time in a local neighborhood there was a practicing witch whose antics we stopped, resulting in her departure from the neighborhood! God did it, for we were not led to pray that. In a near-by shopping area where a totem pole hovered over the parking lot, I was directed to pray it would **rot,** so the enemy couldn't use it. Several weeks passed by when an article appeared in the local newspaper announcing it would be removed because it **was** rotting! Mark 11:24 It has benefited a Christian book store in that locale, for many of the businesses have not survived, nor others which replaced them!

**Very** fruitful and awesome times have also occurred when the Holy Spirit has led me to pray literal **Blood transfusions** of the **living** Blood of Jesus. One woman's blood was too thick and the transfusion changed it pronto, as we spoke to each other on the phone. Another woman was told to medicate for a year, due to trouble with her blood, but when we prayed our faith was interwoven and she saw Jesus pouring His Blood from a pitcher, as the poison went out of her feet. She insisted the doctor take tests the day after our prayer, against strong opposition, and her blood was normal! Alleluia. How wonderful we're allowed to apply His Blood in this manner.

Isn't Almighty God precious to allow and reveal how to pray such exciting things and to know sometimes what the results are! It is so delicious by faith to slam dunk the enemy and blast his evil away! It is particularly precious to know it is the **enemy,** whom we are to tromp on, Luke 10:19 AMP working through **people.** But we are to pray seriously and graciously for the individuals, who may be completely unaware they are being used as a **pawn** by the enemy. Dearly Beloved, I repeat, it is God's **creation** and we choose either favorably to allow **His work** through and in us or the enemy's work in and through us, for there is no **neutral** ground!

# CHAPTER 20

# Despise Not Small Beginnings

One day in my normal reading, when I was attending a "newborn church," the Holy Spirit revealed that there were certain things **every** beginning church should include in order to be **solidly** established on God's Word and principles. Most of us know the most important desire of God is to restore a **living, vital** relationship with **every** person and then change us into the **image** of the Lord Jesus, so the requirement is to redeem everyone! I believe different churches can concentrate on varying aspects of salvation and our growth in Jesus, because of the description of the seven churches in the book of Revelation, chapters 2 and 3, due to our individual callings in the Body of Christ. The cultures and geographic locations can influence what God, Jesus and the Holy Spirit may have to **focus** on at a certain time in greater measure, also!

This revelation came as I was reading my daily portion of the Bible, Ezekiel chapter 16. Several weeks prior to that time, He had shown me the Queen of Sheba, representing the Body of Christ today, had come to ask "hard questions" of King Solomon, 1 Kings 10:1 mirroring our King of kings, Jesus in the New Covenant. Solomon was able to answer "3all her questions; there was nothing so difficult for the king that he could not explain it to her." She told him, "7and indeed the half was not told me. Your wisdom and prosperity exceed the fame of which I heard." Almighty God explained to me that the other half **not told** is **now** released through the Holy Spirit in us and **all** our **hard questions** can be answered. John 14:17, 26 Because it is God's timing and we're living in days much closer to the **return** of King Jesus.

Besides our Abba Father delights in fellowshipping with us, welcomes our questions and **always** delights in answering what we have in our hearts! Countless more persons are listening to God in these days as well. What an immense privilege to live today, to serve God and to know Him intimately, to know the love of Christ experientially, deeply and individually if you desire. Eph. 3:18-19 AMP

With every person who is born anew, faith and willing obedience are indispensable in order to please Father God and grow in His wisdom, understanding and knowledge! Isa. 11:2 So when you accept Jesus as your **Lord** and **Savior,** you will now be Baptized into the Body of Christ and embark as a yielded vessel on the most exhilarating journey of your life, because you have been given a living **eternal Life Line, Jesus!** But we keep deeply loving Jesus and following Him through smooth and rough times. Contrary to the **opinions** of many nonbelievers, it is written that your spirit and soul live forever — in the **light** of God's eternal Life. Rom. 8:29 AMP It was shown at the time probably because of the new church I was attending then. As you study Ezekiel chapter 16 and listen to the Holy Spirit, Dear Readers, keep expecting Him to teach and reveal even more.

We have been made in the image of Almighty God Gen. 1:26-27 and He has made a covenant with us forever, a progression from the covenant initiated with Abram, Gen. 12, 15 who became **Our** Father of Faith. Your parental background is changed Ezek. 16:4 for God transforms **you** into a **new** species of being, 2 Corinth. 5:17 when **you** make Jesus your Lord and Savior. Rom. 10:9-10 The entire chapter of Ezekiel 16 reveals God's love, and we know that He is Love. 1 John 4:8, 16 His Blood cleanses us by eradicating **all** sin, replacing our own blood Ezek. 16:6 with His precious, living, pure and perfect Blood. 1 Pet. 1:19 He protects and adopts us into

His Better Covenant. Heb. As we mature He will **restore, refresh** and **transform** us in spirit, soul and body, and then introduce us to **Abba Father.** John 17; Mark 14:36; Rom. 8:15; Gal. 4:6

He has made **us** the salt of the earth. Ezek. 16:4 "You're here to be salt — seasoning that brings out the God-flavors of this earth. If you lose your saltiness, how will people taste godliness?" Matt. 5:13 The Message Please don't leave this part out of your restoration! Salt acts as a preservative as well, so righteousness, truth, purity, pure joy and respect exemplified by Jesus, are only a few of the things we are to be to the world. Now **we** are salt! The Body of Christ in the church is to be **washed** continually with the water of the Word and fed with the honey of the Word Ezek. 16:19, 4, 9; John 15:3 and anointed (baptized) in the Holy Spirit, Acts 1:5, 7-8; 1 John 2:20, 27 so we will mature. Heb. 13:20-21 Then Jesus will make "us kings and priests to His God and Father." Rev. 1:6

In the Body of Christ as we mature, the Holy Scriptures become so vital, our only Life Line because words are containers of Life or death, as was mentioned! Consequently they have **great** power, for they can be so very encouraging and exciting when certain verses light up! So as we follow **His** assigned reading in our daily walk, our path will be guided in multitudes of situations and a variety of ways.

Very recently a very serious murder case of **thirteen** years ago was resurrected by a book written by the person, though exonerated, believed to be a murderer by many. When the court case was in session, I was praying only in tongues, and leaving the outcome in Father God's hands! He clearly said, **"Mary, My justice in this will be done on earth."** It surely did not seem so then, but God did not elaborate. Now it certainly appears as if the **person** is trapping himself by **wallowing** in his **own** imperfect plans. It is truly written we are our own worst enemy! Isa. 50:11 AMP When this was rekindling my attention, the following verse lit up in my daily reading, Psalm 75:2, AMP "When the proper time is come [for executing My judgments] I will judge uprightly [says the Lord]." Almighty God always will see clearly and surely have His way. Alleluia! Even most recently on the very day thirteen years ago, he was pronounced guilty on twelve criminal counts!

Also **as** we mature we discover everything we need has been given to us in the Better Covenant, because God initiated the **faith covenant** with Abraham to "bless" him and make him "a blessing." Gen. 12:2 With the ads on TV mentioning every minor pain or discomfort you **can** have, a drug is usually recommended. However, the drug may activate **more** side effects than you bargained for from small to immense. My Mother was a small woman and I recall a time when she had taken **one prescribed** pill with a list of side effects numbering **twelve.** One of them started rigor mortis; it was so severe I asked her if she was ready to meet Jesus. The doctor said, "She's just having the list of possible side effects of that pill." Thank God she only took one! This was in the 1970's when fewer dangerous pills were available.

What I'm stressing here is our health, for in Proverbs 4:20-23, in the margin the Word is called our **medicine,** so Dearly Beloved we can walk in Divine Health **daily,** thanks to what our Lord Jesus did on the Cross. In the Old Covenant you can study Deuteronomy 28 and Isaiah 53 in the Amplified Bible. In our New Covenant see 1 Peter 2:24. Earlier I mentioned Almighty God had healed me of migraine headaches. Now I'm bragging about God's tremendous accomplishments to encourage **your** faith!

At first I received healings **unaware** of applying the Word! After I learned **good health** was a gift and our bodies were designed by God to heal themselves, I put **pressure** on applying the Written Word without needing drugs and operations whenever possible! A firm stand in faith was required, from then on any new attacks started from that victory place as faith grew and gained strength. An early illustration was when I attended a weekly meeting at Ethel's to pray together first and I was **definitely ill.** She did say I looked **green.** However, the Holy Spirit helped me press through and total healing came as we praised!

Sometimes I was led by the Lord to alter my diet, water intake or utilize **His** help in changing nonbeneficial habits. The Lord healed me of all of these: Bell's Palsy, migraines, throat polyps, walking pneumonia, double pneumonia, influenza, colds, sore throats, bronchitis, thyroid inactivity, broken wrist for two weeks — **no cast,** one eye with ruptured blood vessel, two cases of shingles — fifty-nine years apart, carbon monoxide poisoning, muscle spasms after injuring a spinal disc, high blood pressure and a **severe** case of sleep apnea! In addition, at ages 36 and 37, two pregnancies even with active emphysema present were problem free. The labor was under four hours for both births. After one attack and some night sweats, when it came time for menopause I quickly told God I'd accept it His way only. His way was once!

Almighty God told me when symptoms start to **decree** an **"R and R" quickly. "Reject the symptoms and Receive the healing! Then immediately take communion."** The manifestation of the healings may not be instantaneous. Keep on declaring only the Word or what He has said until receiving the anointing from the Holy Spirit. We know the **key,** His directions for each of us individually, so **work** your faith muscles in Jesus, as the Written Word. Through the years however, as seasons changed in my life, some symptoms were accepted **wrongly** by me, grew in strength and have become more difficult on my part to receive the manifestations of healing! You can benefit from my mistakes, stay alert and keep **"R and R"** alive!

So keep your flight on the wings of the eagle! Isa. 40:31 Remember how he rests on the currents of wind, remaining dependent on obeying his Maker. Realize how dependent we are on Him and what progress we have made and will continue to do, if we quit not. Recognizing Abba

Father knows best, when He asks us to do perhaps even some seemingly insignificant thing, it will still be a Blessing as Jesus increases in us, if we do it! John 3:30 Love small beginnings!

# CHAPTER 21

# Where and Why His Blood Was Shed!

Because nothing in God's wisdom, knowledge and understanding is flippant or capricious, we often need to stop our **wrong** thinking or our desire to skip down an entangled and unreliable path, probably our own, which can result in a **dead end** or even **danger.** Usually this happens earlier in our walk, as we embark on renewing our minds Rom. 12:2 in obedience to the stability in the Creator of **all** that is and the **unchangeable** Word of Almighty God. 1 Pet. 1:23 As a quick result of growing in the Word and the Lord, because I **did** the Word, I began to realize that our precious Heavenly Father has a **perfect** and **eternal** purpose behind **everything** He does **always.** It is for the **supreme** good for **every** individual born on earth, individually and corporately!

Maybe this will sound simple, but after it became obvious I was **hearing** God clearly in the early 1970's and being led and taught by the Holy Spirit, also by various dynamic teachers, I realized how important it is to not argue about inputs from the Holy Spirit. Once in a while one of them would reveal having done this. I really became aware and truly convinced **God knows a long, long way** beyond and far above me, Isa. 55:8-9 so I determined in reverential honor and respect to Him Isa. 11:2 AMP **not** to turn Him off nor avoid what **might** be distasteful to hear with **no arguing!** We learn by trial and error in the physical realm and in the spiritual realm as well; so sometimes I thought it was He, but it was **not,** but He is patient and knows that is **how** we learn at first. Please do not gloss over this truth, for it must always be in our awareness in our minds, as well as deeply deposited and established in our spirits! This is an all encompassing **inside** truth, so clothe yourself with Jesus outside, too, Col. 2-6-7 because our life is hid in Him! Col. 3:3

In fact I'm reminded of many of the former Godfather's pizza ads on TV in which the godfather said very forcefully at the finish, **"Do it!"** In a later ad a boy who looked like his grandson said, **"Do it!"** to the godfather. My point is? Jehovah God's Holy Word answers that question in John 2:5 when the Mother of Jesus said to the servants, "Whatever He says to you, do *it*." She realized then Her Son alone had the answers! It is the same today, because He **always** depended on Almighty God. He does have **all** the answers for everything and Jesus Himself said "Follow Me" numerous times, which has never been changed. Our part is to work with our Father God by willingly obeying! John 14:21

Truly I am very serious, because it was difficult at first to realize God and Jesus were revealing and enacting the **supreme level** of **Love**, when They agreed in Heaven Jesus would obey God willingly and come to earth as a God Man. The treatment by the people and evil spirits would be dastardly toward Him, before He went to the Cross, on the Cross and afterwards in hell. He had never been separated from His Father, which I believe broke His heart, yet voluntarily in obedience He did as led, as an **absolutely courageous Victor** over everything He did.

This brings me to what the Holy Spirit taught me in the 1980's, when I was asked first to teach a class on the Holy Spirit in one friend's home. Afterwards, other women asked me to teach five classes from Christ's Institute for Ambassadors' syllabus. With permission vital teaching from the Holy Spirit on the Blood of Jesus was added, including the **seven** places where Jesus shed His Blood on the ground and the Cross.

145

Every drop was **profusely** shed and after our Lord Jesus our Victor was resurrected He gathered every drop of It! He delivered It supernaturally to Father God, **alive** and **completely** pure, so It could cleanse things in the Heavenlies. Heb. 9:12 Everything polluted on earth by Adam's decision and behavior had to be **redeemed** from Satan, even the ground. Gen. 3:17 Why are the places recorded? Because of the immeasurable Love and Redemption by Jesus in willing obedience, suffering and selflessness to provide **wholeness** and **wellness** in every facet of our personal lives, individually and corporately, as we obey His ways!

Quite recently Father God told me that one reason Jesus died before the soldiers came to break His legs, was because He was allowed to give up His Spirit prior to the spear piercing His side, which emptied the last of His Blood that spurted out with serum. We are unable to live on earth without the Life of the flesh, the blood, Gen. 9:4 because when it stops flowing we cannot survive!

In Luke 2:21 AMP we learn "And at the end of eight days, when [the Baby] was to be circumcised, He was called Jesus, the name given by the angel before He was conceived in the womb." Did you know that physicians today have learned the least amount of bleeding by an infant occurs on the **eighth** day? **Every** Word in our Bible is recorded for a reason. Mary and Joseph were acting in **perfect** obedience to God, due to His command to Abraham! Gen. 17:10-12 Has it ever occurred to you, dearly Beloved, what an overwhelming responsibility was understood and received, **first** by Mary and then Joseph, raising a Divine Child under extremely unfavorable circumstances from the beginning?

Do you think sometimes **your** path is **too rough?** I have but it's not advisable to "go there" instead **jump** "back on track" and search God's Written Word, while you **say victorious faith** words. "For everyone to whom much is given, from him much will be required; and to whom much has been committed, of him they will ask the more." Luke 12:48 It doesn't take long to find Bible heroes who walked rough pathways in victory — Moses, Joshua, Joseph, Sarah, Hannah, Ruth and Paul to name a few. **We** are **world overcomers;** 1 John 5:4 **millionaires,** hidden in **Christ,** each Blessed beyond measure and re-created with an anointing to be a Blessing to **all** we **contact** because of the **gloriously anointed Victor Jesus!** Ponder and change. Awesome!

Therefore, as a young Man, when Jesus was ministering to the people, the **set time** came for a further portion of the **plan** of **God, not Satan's** (as many have thought through the decades), was to be **revealed!** John 14:28-31 AMP In the Old Testament Joseph was a shadow or type of Jesus because he was mistreated by many — sold as a slave by his brothers, lied against by pharaoh's wife, imprisoned for telling the truth, yet he found favor and became governor in Egypt overnight and helped multitudes in Israel, when they were in famine. Joseph kept in total, deep forgiveness. He told his brothers, when they expected his vengeance against them for their wickedness, "But as for you, you meant evil against me; *but* God meant it for good, in order to bring it about as *it is* this day, to save many people alive." Gen. 50:20

It was also true with Jesus and His countrymen who refused to honor Him. "And they took offense at Him *and* were hurt [that is, they disapproved of Him and it hindered them from acknowledging His authority]; *and* they were caused to stumble *and* fall." Mark 6:3 AMP Jesus said in Mark 6:4, AMP "A prophet is not without honor (deference, reverence), except in his [own] country and among [his] relatives and in his [own] house." In John 7:3-5 AMP we find recorded "5For [even] His brothers did not believe in *or* adhere to *or* trust in *or* rely on Him either." They did not understand nor did they have access to the Written Word in abundance, nor the Holy Spirit as a Living Friend inside, and not the weapons such as the Written Word of God, and the Blood of Jesus. No wonder **far more** is expected of us because **heaps more** have been given to us, as I said! Why would we be centered on ourselves and not be an enormous Blessing to others, for we have been and are continually so overpoweringly Blessed!

This is why we need to consult God to know Him better, for we know not His **big plan,** unless He discloses it; many times it takes even more waiting on Him, especially if He unveils it step by step. Joseph's words were a shadow foretelling what we truly need to understand about the **very evil** treatment of Jesus in His Spirit, Soul and Body! So the places, where His Blood was shed and flowed out from His body, become **extremely significant** to and for us, as each place has a purpose in God's **perfect heart** plan. Then we commence to understand how large God's plan is and the mystery through Jesus of "Christ in you, the hope of Glory," Col. 1:27 as well as the magnitude of His redemption of us, as we meditate and apply His Blood to our lives!

**Firstly,** after His ministry was well under way, as the time for His persecution was nearing, here is a very vivid, accurate account of the start of the agony of Christ and the most difficult events to transpire. Matthew 26 AMP states, "36Then Jesus went with them to a place called Gethsemane, and He told His disciples, 'Sit down here while I go over yonder and pray.' 37And taking with Him Peter and the two sons of Zebedee, He began to show grief *and* distress of mind and was deeply depressed." Luke, the Physician, sees from another aspect, "And being in agony, He prayed more earnestly. And His sweat became like great drops of blood falling down to the ground." Luke 22:44

I am adding a portion of the Greek text of Luke 22 by Wuest, "41And having fallen upon His knees, He was praying, 42saying, 'Father, if you are willing, remove this cup from me. Nevertheless, not my desire but yours, let it keep on being done.' 43And there appeared to Him an angel from heaven, strengthening Him. 44And having entered a state of severe mental and emotional struggle to the point of agony, He was praying more earnestly. And His perspiration became like great drops of blood [by reason of the fact that His blood burst through the ruptured walls of the capillaries, the latter caused by His agony, coloring the perspiration and enlarging the drops] continually falling down upon the ground." See Matthew 26:36-56, Mark 14:32-52 and John 18:1-12. Because of such **severe** agony where the sweat of Jesus became like Blood, this can be counted as the first place **It** was shed!

Jesus came as one hundred per cent Man, also as one hundred per cent God, but He **came** as a **Servant** and in the **likeness of man, humbling Himself totally,** Phil. 2 so it is a true walk of overcoming **all** by doing only what His Father told and showed Him. John 5:19 Therefore this was a **real** struggle, emotionally, mentally and physically! (The Greek here means a conflict as strong as an athletic struggle.) As a result **we** can eagerly follow **God's** will for us, minus a great struggle, for He has taken the **sting** out of it totally, even though at times it may seem complex; then think on Jesus and ask for His yoke for you. In Matthew 11:30 AMP Jesus says, "For My yoke is wholesome (useful, good) — not harsh, hard, sharp, or pressing, but comfortable, gracious, and pleasant; and My burden is light *and* easy to be borne."

You can remember **all** the trials and tribulations Saint Paul went through, too, yet he said Jesus delivered him out of them **all.** 2 Tim. 3:11 He was called by God to prove by a most difficult **faith path** that the Better Covenant does work, Acts 9:15-16 and that he could be entrusted to endure much, because he was **chosen** to write **thirteen** (maybe fourteen) books of the New Testament! How rich spiritually this is for us!

Isaiah prophesied **eight hundred years** before Jesus came to earth, the following: "3He was despised and rejected *and* forsaken by men, a Man of sorrows *and* pains, and acquainted with grief *and* sickness; like one from Whom men hide their faces He was despised, and we did not appreciate His worth *or* have any esteem for Him. 4Surely He

149

has borne our griefs (sicknesses, weaknesses, and distresses) and carried our sorrows *and* pains [of punishment], yet we [ignorantly] considered Him stricken, smitten, and afflicted by God [as if with leprosy]. 10Yet it was the will of the Lord to bruise Him; He has put Him to grief *and* made Him sick. When You *and* He make His life an offering for sin [and He has risen from the dead, in time to come], He shall see His [spiritual] offspring, He shall prolong His days, and the will *and* pleasure of the Lord shall prosper in His hand." Isa. 53 AMP

The Scriptures above are bursting as if pregnant with the many, many restorative achievements Jesus would do during the few days **before, on** and **after** the Cross. The details in the prophecy are **all** inclusive for He was to take upon Himself **all our** sins and griefs for **every** person born — **fear,** unforgiveness, iniquities, pride, hatred, guilt, rejection, abandonment, sorrows, pains, sicknesses, low esteem, broken hearts, the wide range of distresses of the mind, anxieties, shame, concerns, depression, worries, weaknesses, embarrassment, frustrations, pains from punishment and illnesses, wicked name callings, and evil attitudes and thoughts. Abba God's pure, perfect Love chose for our Lord Jesus to endure **all** of this because of His Love for **each** of you. Can you really understand this in your spirit? It requires revelation from Jehovah God to see at least partially how **deeply** He hurt and the **enormous** yet **His perfect** sacrifice because of His **ceaseless** Love for **all** creation!

So when you declare and decree His Blood **cleansing** your minds, your wills and emotions, your brains and intellect with the darkest images in your memory banks, you will learn to abide in the **rest** of **faith** Heb. 4 and in **perfect peace.** Isa. 26:3 But let us rewind because Isaiah lived hundreds of years prior to the set time for Jesus to come to earth!

**Isaiah** prophesied also in verse 5 of chapter 53, AMP "But He was wounded for our transgressions, He was bruised for our guilt *and*

iniquities; the chastisement *needful to obtain* peace *and* well-being for us was upon Him, and with the stripes *that wounded* Him we are healed *and* made whole." Was Isaiah accurate?

**Secondly,** Jesus after praying **alone** three separate times, prepared His disciples by telling them His betrayal was at hand. Matt. 26:46 Judas, a disciple and His betrayer, came with "a detachment *of troops,* and officers from the chief priests and Pharisees" who came "with lanterns, torches and weapons." John 18:3 "Then all the disciples forsook Him and fled." Matt. 26:56 Those who came after Jesus arrested and bound Him. He was taken "to Annas first, for he was the father-in-law of Caiaphas who was high priest that year." John 18:13 Caiaphas "gave counsel to the Jews that it was expedient that one man should die for the people." John 18:14 Luke in chapter 22 writes, here Jesus was **beaten, mocked** and **blasphemed.** Are you seeing and hearing only a minute portion of His shocking abuse for our sakes?

**Thirdly,** Caiaphas, the Jewish scribes, elders, and the whole council finally roused false witnesses against our totally innocent and perfect Lord. When Caiaphas asked Jesus if He was "the Christ, the Son of God," Matt. 26:63 the group collected there were infuriated, because He had kept silent when the false witnesses lied and He also had said if the temple was destroyed in three days, referring to Himself, He would rebuild it. Of course they assumed the physical building.

Then when Jesus said, *"64It is as* you said. Nevertheless, I say to you, hereafter you will see the Son of Man sitting at the right hand of the Power, and coming on the clouds of heaven." Caiaphas accused Jesus of "65blasphemy" and the crowd escalating in violence added that "66He is deserving of death." "67 AMP Then they spat in His face, and struck Him with their fists; and some slapped Him in the face." The Holy Spirit even spoke about this in Isaiah 50:4-11 and verse 6 prophesied this. How perfectly accurate the Bible is because Jehovah God, our King Jesus and the Holy Spirit cannot lie!

**Fourthly,** Jesus was taken to Pilate, the governor, to establish He was King of the Jews. Pilate questioned Him while the crowd escalated stirring up strife. So Pilate asked Jesus if He was the King of the Jews, and He answered him and said *"It is as* you say." Luke 23:3 Openly Pilate said he found **no fault** in Jesus, Luke 23:4 as Jesus kept silent, so he tried to get the Jewish people to take Jesus where they would judge Him by their **own** law!

However, they were **resolute** to pursue having Him killed, so they argued that their law forbids putting any man to death. Pilate again asked Jesus if He was King, thus Jesus made it clear His Kingship was not of this world! John 18:36 Luke 23:5 is the only Gospel that records the chief priests and the multitudes said, "He stirs up the people, teaching throughout all Judea, beginning from Galilee to this place." Pilate, learning He belonged to Herod's authority, sent Him over to Herod, who was in Jerusalem at that time. However, the chief priests and the scribes continued accusing Him vehemently, as Herod and his soldiers mocked and were contemptuous toward Him. So Herod sent Him back to Pilate.

Since Jesus was not being treated physically for all the terrible wounds already inflicted, and was constantly being moved with **open** wounds, which were bleeding and dripping with some oozing profusely, He would be weakening every minute as well. With **all** those deserting Him, His infinite compassion arising within, His heart being broken over separation from His Father and for His Mother and others, He was in an absolutely **indescribable** condition! But He stayed in obedience and in **total trust** in His Father! The very **worst** was yet to come!

**Fifthly,** the custom at the feast was for the governor to release one prisoner chosen by the crowd. So Pilate offered them a notorious murderer, "Barabbas, or Jesus who is called Christ." Matt. 27:17 "But the chief priests and elders persuaded the multitudes that they should ask for Barabbas and destroy Jesus." Matt. 27:20 Pilate still tried to dissuade the crowd but to no avail, so he washed his hands of the Blood of Jesus. The people wanted our precious **Jesus crucified!** Barabbas was released. **Unbelievable,** but **true! God's plan** was still being enforced!

Then the soldiers of the governor took Jesus inside the palace, gathering the whole battalion around Him. Matthew 27:28-30, "28And they stripped Him and put a scarlet robe on Him. 29When they had twisted a crown of thorns, they put *it* on His head, and a reed in His right hand. And they bowed the knee before Him and mocked Him, saying, 'Hail, King of the Jews!' 30Then they spat on Him, and took the reed and struck Him on the head." (The Gospel of John, chapter 19 reveals more conversation regarding Pilate than I've included.)

After they continued to mock Him they took His robe off, put his own clothes back on and led Him off to be crucified! Mark 15:15 declares Pilate had Jesus **scourged** before he released Him to be crucified! *Vine's Expository Dictionary of Biblical Words, New Testament Words, pg 551* describes the Roman way of scourging done to our Lord Jesus: "the person was stripped and tied in a bending posture to a pillar, or stretched on a frame. The 'scourge' was made of leather thongs, weighted with sharp pieces of bone or lead, which tore the flesh of both the back and the breast (cf.. Ps. 22:17)."

Dear Reader, can you see the places on His body, the totally dishonorable treatment to our Lord, a faultless living Man? Because of **where** He was so severely abused in His Soul and Body and where His Blood was shed to redeem your life and sins, what other specific problems or needs in **your daily** living, spirit, soul and body, do you see that He **redeemed** for **you?** You might want to **read** this chapter again from the beginning, concentrating on the paragraph where a number of His accomplishments were listed!

Those things you are accepting as **normal** which can be removed, or emotional hurts you may be nursing, can be eradicated in the New Better Covenant. You might consider depression, name calling, shame over unavoidable situations from others or yourself, before you knew what He had accomplished. From uncomfortable physical ailments to blood abnormalities to brain malfunctions, the list goes on and on. **Many** drugs prescribed for uncomfortable things in our bodies these days are already healed by His stripes. Jesus said let's be diggers in the Word and please our God and Lord by working with the Holy Spirit. "According to your faith let it be to you." Matt. 9:29

**Sixthly,** as He started to carry His Cross, they compelled Simon of Cyrene to take it. Because the custom was to have someone carry the cross to humiliate them or assist in doing so, Jesus apparently carried some of the weight as abused and weakened as He was. Though not specifically stated, it seems obvious that He would shed Blood from the wicked scourging done to His back and the crown of thorns twisted into His skull as He walked to Golgotha, the Place of a Skull. Therefore, His Blood would surely be splattering everywhere on the ground, again, which He would be redeeming from the curse put on it because of Adam's sin!

**Seventhly,** when the soldiers came to Golgotha (in Hebrew), outside the city of Jerusalem, called the Place of a Skull, they crucified Him. John 19:19-20 relates "19Now Pilate wrote a title and put *it* on the cross. And the writing was: JESUS OF NAZARETH, THE KING OF THE JEWS. 20Then many of the Jews read this title, for the place where Jesus was crucified was near the city; and it was written in Hebrew, Greek, *and* Latin."

The procedure followed in crucifixion is historically recorded, so I'm using and summarizing information from *The New Manners & Customs of the Bible pgs 487-489* by James M. Freeman. In Scripture there are more subtle references to much that happened but this is a composite. It was used by the heathen nations as the form of capital punishment. The Jews followed Mosaic Law "by sword, Ex. 21 strangling, fire Lev. 20 and stoning." Deut. 21 Originally "a cross was a wooden pointed stake ... " where just "the heads of captured enemies or criminals" were impaled, then later the entire person was pierced. At first the Greeks and Romans applied it only for slaves; later by the first century it was used for all enemies of the state. pg 487 The Romans used it so often to dissuade evil actions, that it was done regularly by the time Jesus Christ was on earth. pg 488

"According to Jewish law Deut. 21:22-23 offenders 'hung on a tree' were 'accursed of God' and outside the covenant people. Such criminals were to be removed from the cross before nightfall ... ." **Jesus was!** At the time of Jesus the criminal was scourged or flogged because of brutality, to accelerate death and to lessen the criminal's ability to endure the pain. pg 488

"At the site the criminal was often tied (the normal way) or nailed (if greater pain was desired) to the crossbeam. The nail would be driven through the wrist, at the cluster of nerves feeding to the hand, rather than the palm, since the smaller bones of the hand could not support the weight of the body." pgs 488-489 The cross was then planted in the ground, fastened to a pole, and "the feet were tied or nailed also to the post." pg 489 His Blood now flowed from His wrists and from His feet.

At the start Jesus refused any liquid, usually of wine mixed with myrrh, "used to confuse the senses and deaden the pangs of the sufferer," *The New Unger's Bible Dictionary, pg 265* but just before He died a sponge of vinegar was put to His lips. When it was discovered He was dead, a soldier "pierced His side with a spear, and immediately blood and water came out" John 19: 34 — the last place the Blood **flowed!**

**Many** incredible events occurred during this time, reinforced historically, but my focus is on what His Blood has accomplished in His sealed Covenant for enriching and enhancing your life on earth. Psalm 22 reveals He had to have taken embarrassment of all kinds, as He hung there, so severely beaten and in an unrecognizable condition, completely naked, in agonizing pain as He had been for hours, yet in intense compassion thinking of His Mother's care John 19:26-27 before He died, and His Love for us, as I wrote earlier. But there is much, much more.

Beloved Reader, perhaps you might want to look earlier in this chapter at my list, only a fraction of what Jesus as Lord and High Priest accomplished for His Body and for you personally. This is **totally** and really **awesome.** I'm unable to resist the fact that the two criminals crucified on each side of Christ represent salvation powerfully, for one perceived **spiritually** the **truth** and **was saved,** while the second stayed spiritually **blind!** Luke 23:39-43 **Almighty God is working** and **wooing all** the time. Let's **celebrate God, Jesus,** His **Blood** and the **Holy Spirit!**

# CHAPTER 22

# Pleading the Blood of Jesus

Many people are laying their faith aside these days, as it is written, "1Now the Spirit expressly says that in latter times some will depart from the faith, giving heed to deceiving spirits and doctrines of demons, 2speaking lies in hypocrisy, having their own conscience seared with a hot iron!" 1 Timothy 4 This action will cripple everything they do and will certainly not have Almighty God ministering through them, therefore **no** eternal fruit can be produced, no matter how it seems to the world! Why? The Bible says, "But without faith *it is* impossible to please *Him*, for he who comes to God must believe that He is, and *that* He is a rewarder of those who diligently seek Him." Heb. 11:6 "Moreover, everything which is not of faith is sin." Rom. 14:23 Wuest

You are given faith as "the gift of God" Eph. 2:8 but to grow into what Jesus referred to as "great faith," Matt. 8:10 which the Centurion had in the Bible requires **action** on your part. You might be even more convinced when you know that **faith** occurs **243** times in the New Covenant alone! Then **how** does faith come? "Faith is out of the source of that which is heard, and that which is heard [the message] is through the agency of the Word concerning Christ." Rom. 10:17 Wuest Since Jesus the Word became flesh John 1 everything you read and **implant** in your **heart** and **do,** James 1:21-22 truly believing in your heart not only in your mind, will cause and enrich your life and growth spiritually. You will therefore "work out your own salvation with fear and trembling." Phil. 2:12 God saves your spirit and soul but we have a responsibility to develop to be changed into the image of Christ! I do believe in Heaven we will be as if in kindergarten, if we neglect our calling and responsibility here.

"In the New Testament (1) the Greek *Ethnos* in the singular means a people or nation (Matt. 24:7; Acts 2:5; etc.) and even the Jewish people (Luke 7:5; 23:2; etc.). It is only in the plural that it is used for heathen (Gentiles)." *The New Unger's Bible Dictionary, pgs 465-466* We if not Jewish have been grafted into the Vine, Jesus, as descendents of Abraham our Father of Faith, and thankfully we are still in the time of **Grace.** John 15; Rom. 11

So what is faith? I'm giving you an accurate present-day definition. "[1]The fundamental fact of existence is that this trust in God, this faith, is the firm foundation under everything that makes life worth living. It's our handle on what we can't see. [2]The act of faith is what distinguished our ancestors, set them above the crowd. [3]By faith, we see the world called into existence by God's word, what we see created by what we don't see." Heb. 11 The Message

We all want to overcome the world or we would not try to get well if we're ill, nor work to buy food, clothing, cars, many things we even call necessities, which to our ancestors would have been luxuries indeed. We as believers are really working to purchase **seed,** yet faith is still required. It is written "For whatever is born of God overcomes the world. And this is the victory that has overcome the world — our faith." 1 John 5:4

I'm stressing faith so much at this point because of the vital importance of **pleading** the Blood, which many have **discarded, disregarded** or called **old-fashioned.** H.A. Maxwell Whyte said, "As the life of Jesus is in His blood then if we plead, honour, sprinkle and sing about it, we are actually introducing the life of the Godhead (Trinity) into our worship. Our prayers and requests become charged with the life and power of Jesus." (Taken from his **booklet** *The Power of the Blood. pg 30)*

I also know a dear saint now in Heaven, used mightily by God, Darlene Sizemore, who said God commanded her **never** to hold a meeting without singing **at least** one **song** about the **Blood** of **Jesus.** Satan hates the Blood, so do all his spirits, particularly His **religious** ones, so you can understand why singing a powerful song is effective against the enemy! Yippee!

For those you know who are serving the United States of America in the armed forces, Psalm 91 is essential to declare and decree, also asking God for discerning in difficult moments what to do, so a great deal of harm can be avoided. The Scriptures are powerful and alive as is the Blood of Jesus, so apply them all you can. Let us all stay alert! The more you receive revelation about **pleading** the Blood, the more you can apply It wisely!

Before we know the in-depth meaning of pleading the Blood, I'm including two events in the life of Jesus through a very dynamic, petite evangelist, a golden vessel of Almighty God. She ministered in many states in the Midwest, had six children with her first husband, he and their five children graduated to Heaven before her! She traveled by train oftentimes in difficult conditions, was not physically healthy, yet the Ministry of Jesus through her rippled out like an unrestrained, overflowing fountain reaching in power, signs and wonders to a circumference of **10** to **50** miles, changing people and places therein overpoweringly! She had crowds gathering of one to ten thousand, a **most exceptional** occurrence in the mid-1800s! Her meetings varied in length sometimes from 9:00 a.m. until midnight or she held sometimes as many as three meetings daily.

"I next went to Summitville, Indiana, and commenced meeting on Wednesday evening, February 25, 1885. The house was crowded the first night. The crowd was made up of infidels, skeptics and scoffers. Many of these scoffers were church members. A few of God's children stood by me praying for victory. Most everyone said, 'She will make a failure here,' and were hoping it would be a failure. I went in the strength of God, knowing that He that was for me was more than those who were against me. I arose and told them that God was coming in power, that many of them would be at the altar that night, crying for mercy. I saw some laughing, as if to say, you do not know us. I began singing, "Let Me in the Lifeboat." The Holy Spirit fell upon me. God made them be able to see the lifeboat on the ocean of eternity, and them drifting away into darkness and despair, down to an awful hell. I led in prayer. When I arose, the silence of death reigned over the house. They were trembling under conviction. While I was preaching, God sent every word like arrows, dipped in the blood of Jesus, to their hearts."

*Signs and Wonders, pg 57,* by Maria Woodworth-Etter

Another exciting event happened at The Stone Church in Chicago in 1913! "It was marvelous how God brought all the different Pentecostal missions together. I never permit any doctrinal points, no 'isms,' no antagonistic points, to be aired or brought up in my meetings; nothing but Christ, and Him crucified, and the Resurrection. They soon understand and get their eyes off one another, forget their ideas and differences, begin to love one another, and soon feel the need of getting deep in God. It was glorious to have so many ministers, evangelists, and workers from everywhere coming like little children to the feet of Jesus to be refilled for better service; the watchword was 'Go forward.' We all felt we must get deeper in God, the need of more power from on high; of special qualifications from the Lord, of gifts and wisdom and discerning of spirits. They became hungry for more of God. Their very flesh cried out for God. We prayed for hundreds of those ministers and workers with the laying on of hands, and the power of the Holy Spirit fell on all. Many fell and lay at the feet of Jesus, like the prophets and apostles of old. They had visions of heaven and saw things to come; they believed what the Lord Jesus had said of the Spirit of God: *'He will show you things to come'* (John 16:13). Many received gifts and special calls." *pg 260*

"The conviction was so deep that scores of believers came out from the audience wanting the laying on of hands and prayer. There were too many. So the Lord showed me that if they all would come and stand before the pulpit, He would bless them. I told all hungry souls to gather around and give themselves to God for everything and anything: we would stand and sprinkle the blood of the everlasting covenant, the blood of the Lamb, on them, and then God would pour out His Spirit and give them blessing and gifts. I asked several of the most God-filled ministers to stand with me in faith and prayer. Oh, it was wonderful how the cloud of glory and power came down! Many staggered and fell; the power swept all over the house. This was something new; no one had ever seen anything like it. Many were saved and healed. Surely the power of the Lord was present to heal, save, and give gifts. He honored His Word and our faith. The Word must be demonstrated." *pg 260*

The dear lady to whom I refer is Maria Woodworth-Etter who kept written records of her own sermons, as well as compiling them all. Considering what a forerunner she was to the happenings and revelations today, I find her a yielded, dedicated and willingly obedient and awesome example of courage and perseverance, even more so since she ministered when women were **unwelcome** in the pulpit! May we be so deeply in love with Him that we completely trust our Heavenly Father by doing **all** that He's asked or commanded us. That all we accomplish is done only unto Him to **please just Him!** Jesus said, "Without Me you can do nothing." John 15:5

Now, can you with the help of the Holy Spirit imagine a courtroom filled with many persons, who are all obedient to Almighty God, and where perfect justice reigns because a wise and righteous Judge is currently presiding and **you** are in the courtroom? Perhaps thinking of Solomon and the book of Proverbs, because of God's wisdom deposited in him, will instigate painting this picture in your mind quickly. Continue by thinking of a person you dearly love who is coming before the Judge because of a crime he committed and is **tormented** with fear, but who **has repented** of all his sins, **believed** and **received** Jesus in his heart and declared Him as Lord! Therefore having been "born again" John 3:15-16 he has been made "a creation new in quality" in Christ Jesus! 2 Corinth. 5:17 Wuest "And there are three that bear witness on earth: the Spirit, the water, and the blood; and these three agree as one." 1 John 5: 8 "And the Spirit is the One who is constantly bearing witness, because the Spirit is the truth." 1 John 5:6 Wuest (a Greek scholar)

Present there in the Heavenly Court are Almighty Jehovah God, The King of kings, Jesus, Who is interceding as our High Priest as well, Rom. 8:34 and also the Intercessor in us on earth, the Holy Spirit. "For there are three who bear witness in Heaven: the Father, the Word, and the Holy Spirit; and these three are one." 1 John 5:7 But you see the living Blood of Jesus is present also, as a **Witness** because It is alive and has been present prior to man's arrival! When the blood of animals was put on the doorposts in the Old Testament, it was foretelling protection against death by Jesus' Blood in every respect for eternity. It also foretold the Cross with Blood on two sides representing His hands and the top of His head with blood dripping down forming a cross! In addition we have His Word engraved on our **hearts.** Heb. 8:10 **All** are there to administer justice perfectly for your friend!

What has given that person such Love and Power? Acceptance of the Lord Jesus Christ in his heart, Eph. 3:17 belief in His Perfect Lordship,

His Living Blood and that He is God's Word personified. Did you already know Heaven is presided over in this way? Besides, **all** the Laws and Statutes are faultless. Mistakes are **impossible** — for **all** that is said and done is **Truth!**

Here the reality is we can **plead** the Blood of Jesus because It has prepared the way for **every single one** of us, since Jesus shed **all** of His, gleaned It, transported It, sprinkled It in Heaven, Heb. 9 where It is living, and speaking forgiveness and "mercy triumphs over judgment." James 2:13 In the Old Testament the blood of the sacrificed, perfectly healthy animals was sprinkled on the "mercy seat of pure gold," Exod. 25:17 pointing to Jesus The Lamb and the **value** of His Blood unknown then! The blood of animals was atop the ark and there God said He would "meet" and "speak intimately" with Moses. Exod. 25:22 AMP This reveals God's heart again regarding the importance of **blood** even prior to revealing His Master plan for the Blood of Jesus throughout the Bible from Genesis through Revelation. Also, the precious Blood of Jesus is what prepares the way so we are commanded to "come boldly to the throne of grace." What an astounding Gift!

It seems for those who **object** about pleading the Blood, either discount It or are perhaps confused. Some think "plead" means to beg. **No,** not at all. In reference to Romans 11:2 the Greek states "the verb means to meet with, then to meet with the purpose of conversation, to have an interview with, to plead with or accuse." *Linguistic Key to the Greek New Testament,, pg 372* The meanings of **plead** in Hebrew in the Old Testament parallel with words such as "contend," "strive," and "plead my cause" with those in the New Testament. Psa. 35:1; 1 Sam. 24:15 In Almighty God's **view** and **reality** no one can contend or strive against Jesus, so obviously His Blood will be in total harmony and therefore we can plead our cause, as It has already gone before us! So we "come boldly to the throne of grace," Heb. 4:16 where we're reconciled back to Father God because there's "peace through the blood of His cross." Col. 1:20

When Satan and his angels were flung out of Heaven to earth, Saint John "10heard a loud voice saying in heaven, 'Now salvation, and strength, and the kingdom of our God, and the power of His Christ have come, for the accuser of our brethren, who accused them before our God day and night, has been cast down. 11And they overcame him by the blood of the Lamb and by the word of their testimony, and they did not love their lives to the death.' " Rev.12

Because the Life of our soul and body is in our blood and the Life of the Body of Christ **spiritually** is in the Blood of Christ, it is as a glorious symphony of eternal perfection for the seizing! Yes, after repentance, we have consequences to accept for our actions sometimes but **only** God decides, forgives and proceeds from there, for let us remember our sins when confessed are eradicated, 1 John 1:7-9 and **only** Father God has the answers. Glory!

The most difficult **roadblock** for you **may be** to forgive **yourself!** It becomes **amazingly** easier, when you know Abba Father **forgives** and also **forgets** Heb. 8; 10 every confessed sin about which you may still be brooding. **He** alone is qualified to determine any judgment and results. God has based this world on infallible laws which are perfectly just, righteous and unable to fail. Heaven is really like a Perfect Courtroom, no lying, so no false accusations because everything is decided flawlessly.

Dear Reader, no person has all of the truth, even Saint Paul said that, so consult the Holy Spirit if you fail to sense an inner witness from Him when applying the Scriptures, but do check the Bible! Can you keep an open mind and even bypass it at times when studying them, prior to drawing your own conclusions and then perhaps missing out on His revelation?

# CHAPTER 23

# Enriched? Understand Covenant Steps

In a sense recognizing the **steps** in the covenant to **seal it** in you helps one understand in greater **depth** the **magnitude of the Better Covenant!** Father God and Jesus cutting it together for **you** personally is almost unfathomable! It reveals victorious features of **daily living now** for each person, plus the **eternal** meaning as well. In addition, the meaning of taking communion is greatly enhanced to **amplify** and **keep alive** promises packaged in the covenant God and Jesus have given. You can halt undesirable habits, as well as honor burning decisions between Daddy God and you whenever and as often as you require.

Jehovah **God came** to Abram, saying, "2I will make you a great nation; I will bless you and make your name great; and you shall be a blessing." Gen. 12 As time passed "the word of the Lord came" to him "in a vision saying, 'Do not be afraid, Abram. I *am* your shield, your exceedingly great reward.' " Gen. 15:1 So since Almighty God **initiated** a Blessing Covenant **in Blood** then we should **know** the importance of the steps. The sources I've studied through the years have disagreed about **the order,** but **not** about the steps themselves, so we'll avoid legalism by just naming them.

I do suggest here a fascinating and accurate booklet to enrich your appreciation, titled *The Blood Covenant* by E.W. Kenyon with over 31 printings. It relates the truth of H.M. Stanley in Africa, a journalist and explorer there, in the mid and late 1800s. He was **not** accomplishing what he went to do, until he met and cut covenant with **one** tribal chieftain in particular when he **learned** its importance! He traveled all over Africa cutting covenants with almost forty others successfully. In fact, I truly believe his persistence and love of the Africans is why revival through the evangelist Reinhard Bonnke and others is so constant there. God has made people free of independent and self-made persons, hatred and prejudice!

Through his vessel Paul, prejudice **should end** readily forever because the Holy Spirit said in Acts 17, "24God, who made the world and everything in it, since He is Lord of heaven and earth ... 25gives to all life, breath and all things. 26And He has made from one blood every nation of men to dwell on all the face of the earth," so marriage is acceptable between different races for the important requirement in the heart of God is to be **equally yoked — a male believer marries a female believer!** 2 Corinth. 6:14

The covenant between God and His creation, you, and between two people or families, **extending** for generations, is usually based on their strengths and weaknesses, exchanging and helping the other person where you are stronger and he or she helps you where you're weaker. In the Old Testament King David and Jonathan, Saul's son, had a pure covenant together with God. Even after Jonathan was killed, King David searched out an **heir** until he found his crippled son, Mephibosheth, to continue to keep their covenant! 2 Sam. 9

A marriage ordained by God can really display this when each partner is willing to **submit** to the other and as a couple **submit** to the **Lordship** of Jesus. Eph. 5 The covenant of God and Jesus however on our part is receiving all and returning true love in thankfulness by allowing Jesus the Christ to **live** and have **His way** through us! We are the

Body of Christ with One Head, Jesus, so in the bigger picture each of us is **one** in **Him** and in covenant with everyone within the Body! When we really participate then Jesus, our elder Brother, calls us **friend,** a **covenant** word. Prov. 18:24; John 15:14-15

Briefly here are the steps included. Covenant truly means **all** I own is yours! In Israel the blessings and curses would be boldly declared from separate mountain tops! The Blessings were spoken from Mt. Gerizim and the curses from Mt. Ebal. Deut. 27 They are listed in Deuteronomy 28. I've heard people who've visited Israel tell how far their own voices would carry, when they'd call out, so the people when Jesus was on earth would surely have heard all that was spoken. Since Jesus was made a **curse,** Gal. 3:13-14 **if you** are **His** you need **no curses** ever plaguing you. Your responsibility is to stay in integrity of heart **believing** and **trusting wholly** Almighty God.

David and Jonathan probably did all these steps, so let's imagine them for better understanding! We know from covenant talk and some detail in the Bible. 1 Sam. 17; 18 They **exchanged garments** or **coats,** symbolizing the **authority** given back and forth and accepted by each other. Luke 10:19-20 Remember the beautiful tunic Jacob gave Joseph? It was a shadow of authority and favor that we received through God to Jesus to us as sons if we're Spirit led! Gen. 37:3 This reveals a shadow of the accomplishments of Jesus prior to His total Victory on the Cross, yet given to us. God and Jesus did this, because they cut a perfect unbreakable covenant and **after** Jesus defeated our enemy and his followers, He gave **us** His **authority** and **power** over **all** of them! Mark 16

They **exchanged weapons** or **belts,** symbolizing the sword, armor, bows and arrows. It meant each one would receive **all** of each other's strength and support in daily living. You have the total armor of **light** of and in Jesus, Rom. 13:12; Eph. 6:11, 14-17; 1 Thess. 5:8 so you **can** receive **all** of God's strength and support and His standing for you and pledging His support. Isa. 43 You may be saying to yourself, "but that was for the Hebrews and Abraham and his descendants." Very true but we have been grafted into the Vine (Jesus) and receive the promises in faith for our lives, because Jesus is **the Seed** and what **He did was done for us!** The Living only true God will not forsake His children living in the Better Covenant.

To continue, cutting is done on the wrist or the palm of each other, then you mingle your blood, making you "blood brothers." Shedding the blood seals the covenant for the scar is a permanent testimony to the covenant! Usually a substance like gun powder or ashes is put on the cuts to keep them permanently visible! Some covenants require drinking the blood; but **God forbids it** because of the **life in** the blood. Gen. 9:3-4; Lev. 17:10-14

You do not have to cut covenant, for you have already been spiritually cut when you allowed your heart to be circumcised in water baptism, "by putting off the body of the sins of the flesh, by the circumcision of Christ, buried with Him in baptism." Col. 2:11-12 You have been given a New Spirit and a new heart by God! Ezek. 36:26-27 We are to "have no confidence in the flesh" and "worship God in the Spirit." Phil. 3:3

Each step is vital but **walking in blood** is imperative! It is vividly described in Genesis 15 and scholars believe that both **God** and **Jesus** appeared to **Abram,** because of the "smoking oven and a burning torch" passing "between those pieces." God commanded that Abram bring a heifer, a goat, a ram (each three years old) and a turtledove and a pigeon. Excluding the birds he was told to cut each animal down the middle, placing each piece opposite each other! When Abram was asleep, God and Jesus appeared unto him with an awesome revelation of the future. In the covenant **step** the two friends would start in the middle walking in the Blood, making a figure eight because there is no beginning or end. This emphasizes eternal unbroken promises!

They would **exchange names** which is discussed in Chapter Four. As a **believer** we are richer yet for we are called by the **anointed Name** of our **Lord, Christian,** and then are commanded in His Name, **Jesus!** So you see the **beyond bountiful** nature of Father God, not naming us **Jesus,** which is **above every** name, but we receive His **Anointed Name** thus becoming anointed, 1 John 2:20, 27 when we follow His command to be Holy Spirit Baptized! Luke 24:49 That **inestimable gift** enables us to accomplish and accomplish and accomplish "20exceedingly abundantly above all that we ask or think, according to the power that works in us, 21to Him *be* glory in the church by Christ Jesus throughout all ages, world without end. Amen." Eph. 3:20-21 We are to do "greater works than" Jesus, John 14:12 and all revealed in Mark 16:15-18! Alleluia Forever!

The last step is a **covenant meal,** so when the entire family or elders are present they would get together for a covenant meal. The "blood brothers" would eat together, feeding wine and bread to each other; if the people were not Hebrew they used bread and blood. I believe husband and wife at the wedding reception feeding each other cake represents the covenant.

To me the Last Supper would represent this covenant meal before we get to Heaven when Dr. Luke said, "19And He took bread, gave thanks and broke *it,* and gave *it* to them, saying, 'This is My body which is given for you; do this in remembrance of Me.' 20Likewise He also *took* the cup after supper, saying, 'This cup *is* the new covenant in My blood, which is shed for you.' " Luke 22 This must have been a **mystery** to them for that was **verboten,** yet here was their Friend and Lord telling them they were eating His body and drinking His Blood! To me since Jesus was and is the Word made flesh among us, this is spiritually eating His Words and drinking His Life. Ask the Holy Spirit for we do know at Passover the origin of communion was birthed!

# CHAPTER 24

# Victory in Christ for You!

Dearly Beloved Reader, my heart is **still** pouring forth such an unfathomable persistent yearning for Daddy God's **presence** to **saturate** your entire spirit, soul and body, with His unconditional **Love** — *hesed, agapé* — for there is **nothing** purer, more glorious or gracious available **anywhere** on earth! He loves you as you are at this very moment, no matter what you are doing, have done, or even what you're thinking. But because Almighty God knows what's best for you He has to have **yielded partnership** from you.

Early on after I was Baptized in the Holy Spirit, He drew my attention to the Greek meaning shown in the Amplified version of the Bible that "believe" means far more than accept as true! This helps to keep in our hearts whenever we think of the Trinity. John 3:16, "For God so greatly loved *and* dearly prized the world that He [even] gave up His only-begotten (unique) Son, so that whoever believes in (trusts, clings to, relies on) Him shall not perish — come to destruction, be lost — but have eternal (everlasting) life."

We **do** follow His ways in obedience to receive blessings from Him in order to be the Blessing He meant for every one of us to be! Then our lives become so peaceful, joyful and literally shine forth, that others will see evidence that we **are** transformed! It is like we're in a cocoon of purified hidden talents, attitudes and anointings that become converted into **totally untainted beauty,** inside-out, His Image, "which is Christ in you, the Hope of glory!" Col. 1:27 Our life hidden, actually I believe **consumed** by His presence. His Love pouring through you **triumphs** over all problems and **cannot fail.** 1 Corinth. 13:8

Will you ask our Great Jehovah what He has refreshed, reinforced or revealed to **you** through reading the **Scriptures,** so His Glory will shine brightly through your entire being as the Light of His Word consumes the darkness? Would you see with your "inside out" faith zoom lenses, standing beneath the Cross of Jesus alone with Him, while His Glorious Words beam forth as a fountain spraying all over you of **love** and **forgiveness?** Ezek. 36:25-28 He **sees you** through the **Blood** of Jesus applied on your spirit, soul and body! His Words **still** flood the atmosphere "Father, forgive them, for they do not know what they do." Luke 23:34 Therefore, we forgive ourselves, where we have failed doing right, repent because we love Him and press ahead on His path for us! Phil. 3:12-14

So I exhort you to personally honor and respect His precious Blood **daily** and **know,** being "fully persuaded" that the "20God of peace ... through the blood of the everlasting covenant, 21make you complete in every good work to do His will, working in you what is well pleasing in His sight, through Jesus Christ, to whom *be* glory forever and ever. Amen." Heb. 13 By His Grace we are becoming a Blessing wherever we go as He blesses us, **totally Victorious in Christ!**

### My Blood, My Blood, You Must Know!

Understanding, honoring and appreciating the Blood these Last Days must come.
Acknowledge My Ways — the path is clear, the power great,
But only if the Blood is honored in high estate.
Don't just think it — hear it aloud — for it will disperse many a cloud!

Mary, often it's contrary to what people, my own even, will do,
But it must be applied consistently and proclaimed by you.
Keep declaring, decreeing wherever you go about My Blood.
Oh, Body of Christ — **you** must know.

Don't cast it aside or treat it lightly;
In the morning apply and yes, especially nightly!
The Blood is **alive** with power encased to be utilized —
Delivering, protecting the human race.

It will always and forever be,
But It's been a part of My Plan always, can't you see?
Sing! Shout! Tell wherever you go!
**My Blood, My Blood — you must** know!

Prophecy by Mary Anna Burriss (February 20, 1997)

# Songs

### The Blood of Jesus is Alive!

The Blood of Jesus is alive, it's living and it's powerful,
The Blood of Jesus is alive, it contains the Life of God.

The Blood contains the Life of Jesus Christ my Lord,
My Deliverer, my Healer, my Redeemer, Almighty God!

So demons scream and have to flee and sickness has to go
Because the Blood of Jesus is alive, It contains the Life of God!
Yes, It contains the Life of God!

Song by Teresa Sjolander

# Songs

## *What a Healing Jesus*

When walking by the sea, "Come and follow Me," Jesus called
Then all through Galilee, the sick and the diseased, He healed them all
Jesus hasn't changed, His power is just the same as when He walked the shore
This God of yesterday is still the healing Jesus, now and evermore

What a healing Jesus I found in You
What a healing Jesus, You restore, refresh and renew
You're my healing Jesus, for such a time as this
Arise on healing wings, Son of righteousness

The Spirit of the Lord now is upon me, anointed me
To heal the broken hearts, open prison doors, set captives free
To comfort those that mourn, fill their lips with praise, to pour the oil of joy
That they may become the trees of righteousness
The planting of the Lord

What a healing Jesus I found in You
What a healing Jesus, You restore, refresh and renew
You're my healing Jesus, for such a time as this
Arise on healing wings, Son of righteousness

What a healing Jesus I found in You
What a healing Jesus, You restore, refresh and renew
You're my healing Jesus, for such a time as this
Arise on healing wings, Son of righteousness

You're here on healing wings, Son of righteousness.

Mary Y. Brown
ASCAP

# The Blood Line

My God is Love, He created man to pour His love into
But the rebel choice and fall made that impossible to do
He longed for someone more to choose His love and will,
Let His light shine through
From the dawning of eternity God wanted each of us in His family.

 Chorus:
So He placed a Blood Line around the family
Issued from the heart of Father God
It overflowed at Calvary, a Blood Line to stand for all eternity
The Blood that gives us access to the throne
The power of the Blood will bring us home.

Because our God is Love He always planned for you to pour His Love into
But the rebel choice and fall made that impossible to do
He just wants you to choose His love and will,
Let His Light shine through
From the dawning of eternity God wanted you in His family.

 Chorus:
So He placed a Blood Line around the family
Issued from the heart of Father God
It overflowed at Calvary, a Blood Line to stand for all eternity
The Blood that gives us access to the throne
The power of the Blood will bring us home.

Lord, most of us bear prodigals upon our hearts in prayer
They just need to know You, Jesus and surrender to Your care
We pray that they would choose Your love and will,
Let Your Light shine through
From the dawning of eternity You prepared a place for each of them in Your family.

 Chorus:
So we place a Blood Line by faith around our family
Issued from the heart of Father God
It overflowed at Calvary, a Blood Line to stand for all eternity
The Blood that gives us access to the throne
The power of the Blood, the power of the Blood,
The power of the Blood will bring them home.

The power of the Blood will bring them home,
Will bring us home Lord, You bring us all home.

Lynn Crawford

# Shedding of the Blood of Jesus

He cried out, "Father, not My will but Yours!"
As drops of Blood poured from His pores
Seven times He paid the price, by the shedding of Blood
For His chosen Bride
He took a beating that marred His face
For the ugliness of sin He paid the price
Seven times He paid the price, by the shedding of Blood
For His chosen Bride
They crowned Him with thorns, the poisonous kind
That Blood paid for my carnal mind
Seven times He paid the price, by the shedding of Blood
For His chosen Bride
While man laid stripes on the Son of God
With the Blood that flowed my healing was bought
Seven times He paid the price, by the shedding of Blood
For His chosen Bride
The Cross He was made to carry uphill
Caused more Blood to flow and It flows for me still
Seven times He paid the price, by the shedding of Blood
For His chosen Bride
Blood from the nails piercing His feet and His hands
Washed my walk and works satisfying God's demands
Seven times He paid the price, by the shedding of Blood
For His chosen Bride
On the Cross water and Blood flowed from His side
He had given His all for the church to arise
Seven times He paid the price, by the shedding of Blood
For His chosen Bride
So rejoice, O' Bride, rejoice
By lifting up your voice
For the Lamb is now your Risen King
Let's shout, let's dance, let's sing

Glory, glory to our King
Victory, victory we have in Him
Holy, Holy is He alone,
The Risen Christ now reigning from His throne

Katrin Hoffman

# How to Receive Salvation
## (Spirit within) John 14:16-17

1. Do you believe in God?

2. Do you believe in Jesus?

3. Do you believe Jesus died for your sins?

4. If you died now would you be with the Lord?

5. Would you like to know for sure?

   **Vitally important:  Ask for forgiveness and specifically renounce your involvement with cults and the occult.**
   (See Deuteronomy 18:10-12; Galatians 5:19-21)

   Ask God for a strong Christian to help you with questions you may have and to assist you in finding a church.


# Salvation Scriptures

**Romans 10:9-10** ...    Declare **aloud** Jesus is Lord.
                        Believe in your heart God raised Him from the dead.

| | | |
|---|---|---|
| **1 John 5:13** | ... | **You can know for sure!** |
| **John 3:16** | ... | **His love** for us!! |
| **John 10:10** | ... | **Abundant life** for you! |
| **Romans 3:23** | ... | Our **problem** — you and I — is **sin.** |
| **Romans 6:23** | ... | Sin separates us from God. |
| **James 2:10** | ... | One sin is enough. |
| **John 14:6** | ... | Only **one** way! |
| **1 Timothy 2:5** | ... | **One Mediator!!** |

**Prayer:** Dear Almighty God, forgive me for all my sins. I take You at Your Word that You forgive those who ask. I believe in my heart that Jesus died for me, was buried and rose on the third day, and now sits at Your right hand, Father. Jesus I ask you to be my Lord, as You are my Savior. I give myself to You. I honor Your Blood Jesus, which now protects me and eradicates my confessed sins! Colossians 1:19-20; 1 John 1:9 I have asked and believe Father God that You have saved me. Thank You for being faithful, in Jesus' Name.

# How to Receive the Baptism of The Holy Spirit
## (Spirit upon) Acts 1:8

**(a separate experience** from being Born Again) **Acts 8:14-17**

**Must answer "Yes" to:**

1. If you died in the next few hours, would you be with the Lord?
   **John 14:16-18**

2. Are you ready for this new power that will fill your life?

   Power to witness **Acts 1:8**

   Must be thirsty to receive. **John 7:37-38**

   **Now, renounce any** involvement with cults or the occult.

   Please read instructions regarding Salvation.

3. The Bible says you will be baptized with the Holy Spirit the very moment
   you ask **in faith.**

   Do you believe that? **Luke 11:13, 9-10; Mark 11:24**

4. The Bible says you will respond **after** being baptized in the Holy Spirit by
   speaking in tongues. Do you believe that? **Mark 16:17; Acts 10:44-46**

5. Will **you** speak in tongues **by faith** right away as we pray? **Acts 19:2-6**

**Prayer:** Father in Heaven, I believe Jesus Christ is my Baptizer and this gift is
mine just for the asking. I believe I will begin to speak in a new language I've
never known, immediately after I pray. I need this power in my life. I will coop-
erate totally with You from this moment on in faith. I ask You in the Name of
Jesus, baptize me **now.** I have received!! Thank You for giving me new power
and the ability to speak praises to You now in a way I've never learned. Amen
in Jesus' Name.

Both of these outlines are based on those of John Decker, a teacher and evangelist, with additions from my experience.

# ABOUT THE AUTHOR

At eighty-four years of age, Mary Anna Burriss has more than forty years ministry experience in the United States, Scotland, and Latvia, with an emphasis on teaching, prophesying and phone prayer counseling.

When Jesus baptized her in the Holy Spirit, He became her teacher. God's perfect will replaced His good and acceptable will—including revelation and application of the Blood of Jesus.

She is also the author of *The Victor's Mind Can Be Yours* (hardcover, $14.99). In this book she candidly shares experiences of her own growth process and scriptural insight on how to change old patterns of thought and speech to become Christ minded and the rewards of doing so. Topics covered include:

> —Is meekness weakness?

> —God's 8 R's to a renewed mind

> —How to avoid spiritual cancer

> —Our golden nuggets

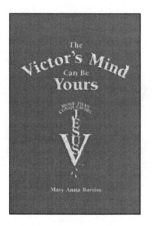

To order your copy of *The Victor's Mind Can Be Yours* or additional copies of *The Blood Reigns Forever* contact your local bookstore, Barnes & Noble, amazon.com or use the address below.

If this book has touched your life, Mary would love to hear from you.

You can write to her at:

Mary Anna Burriss
PMB814
15600 N.E. 8th Street, Suite B1
Bellevue, WA 98008

# Notes

# Notes

# Notes

# Notes

# Notes

# Notes